# Think like an Entrepreneur

## THE MINDSET OF SUCCESS

## Jane Mara

ACCLAIMED AUTHOR OF
**INTUITION ON DEMAND**

First published 2017

By Expert Intuition Pty Ltd

GPO Box 2410, Sydney, NSW 2001 Australia

www.janemara.com

© Jane Mara, 2017

This book is copyright. All rights reserved. No part of this publication may be reproduced, stored in a retrieval system, or transmitted in any form or by any means, electronic, mechanical, photocopying, recording or otherwise, without the prior written permission of the publisher.

**National Library of Australia Cataloguing-in-Publication entry**

Creator: Mara, Jane, author.

Title: Think Like an Entrepreneur : The Mindset of Success / Jane Mara.

ISBN: 9780646974408 (paperback)

ISBN: 9780646974415 (ebook)

Subjects: Mara, Jane.

       Business

       Psychology

       Entrepreneurship

       Success

       Mindset

Cover design by Alexandre Law Min, Outcome Life

Typesetting by eMatti

Printed and bound by IngramSpark in Australia

# Think like an Entrepreneur

## THE MINDSET OF SUCCESS

# Jane Mara

ACCLAIMED AUTHOR OF
**INTUITION ON DEMAND**

This book is dedicated to all the serial entrepreneurs in the world who have ever been told - Get a job!

YOU KNOW WHO YOU ARE!

# Contents

| | |
|---|---|
| Foreword | i |
| Research Questionnaire | vii |
| Acknowledgements | ix |
| Introduction | 1 |
| CHAPTER 1: The Science of Entrepreneurial Mindset | 7 |
| CHAPTER 2: The Frequency of Opportunity | 25 |
| CHAPTER 3: The Power of Beliefs | 37 |
| CHAPTER 4: The Energy of Passion | 47 |
| CHAPTER 5: The Role of the Heart | 59 |
| CHAPTER 6: Focused Intention | 73 |
| CHAPTER 7: The Mindset of Success | 83 |
| Afterword | 91 |
| References | 93 |
| About the Author – Jane Mara | 97 |
| Contact Details | 99 |

# Foreword

Introducing Jane Mara – by Emeritus Professor Murray Gillin

 *Intuition, that essential leadership ability to apply not just technical expertise but also wisdom in making business decisions, comes naturally to the self aware leader.*

DANIEL GOLEMAN 2002

From my many years of research, I would define an entrepreneur as a person who has a clear vision of what is to be created and is passionately committed to the implementation of the opportunity. This opportunity or vision may defy current rational thinking and invariably challenges accepted business models.

How does an entrepreneur or team of entrepreneurs create successful new business concepts or opportunities? My research from the HeartMath Institute® in the USA and in collaboration with the Australian Graduate School of Entrepreneurship at Swinburne University of Technology in Melbourne delivers an extraordinary answer drawing extensively on an understanding of the human autonomic nervous system and quantum physics. This research forms the basis of what is being presented to you in this book.

Jane Mara came to my attention in early 2008, as a result of her desire to learn more about intuition and my research into the human ability to involve the entire psycho-physiological system in processing intuitive perception. Jane was able to bring a 'real life' dimension to this work through her successful consultancy business. Indeed she is a true practitioner and seeks to integrate theory and practice in her research and consulting.

Jane has a number of distinctive characteristics and capabilities relevant to this type of work. She is an intuitive, innovative thinker, entrepreneurial and curious – and she practices what she preaches. She has used these skills to weave together theory and practice, big picture strategy and detail execution, for herself and the people she works with. She has lots of that vital entrepreneurial characteristic – tenacity.

This is demonstrated by her study of intuition in management that extends over years. When she first commenced this work, intuition was viewed with a great deal of scepticism by many people in the corporate world.

Jane has a solid international career in business, dealing with strategic planning, brand and marketing management, including management of a specialist marketing group in the financial services industry.

Her work capably covers four distinct areas which she integrates very effectively – research on the role of intuition in management, specifically in entrepreneurial management; applying research findings to 'evangelising', developing and presenting management training programs and advisory/mentoring to management.

# FOREWORD

Jane has been rigorous in researching the literature and in undertaking field work. Jane has sought findings and information in Australia about the science and practice of entrepreneurship and its relationship to intuition with limited results. Subsequently, she travelled to UK and USA to interview and research entrepreneurial thinkers. She documented over 50 case studies in these three countries covering management in business, the arts, public services and the professions. These studies and her conclusions were then incorporated into her first book, *Intuition on Demand*, published in 2006. Her ability to present her topic with clarity led to her first book being recognised by *AFR Boss* magazine as one of the 50 Top Management books for 2006.

Importantly much of her research has focused on seeking an understanding of how successful repeat entrepreneurs integrate intuition and intentionality into recognizing opportunities for business innovation and development.

These repeat entrepreneurs are essential to the creation of new ventures and the resulting job opportunities within the community. An essential outcome of this work has resulted in a program to apply this new knowledge to the development of improved comprehension and confidence amongst managers and senior executives to use intuition as a major element in decision making.

Jane has continued to source both leading overseas research learning about a number of techniques that provide electro-physiological measures of intuitive behaviour. Integrating these developments into her consultancy practice has helped executives measure their own performance.

Her record of facilitating intuitive learning programs with leading corporate companies, her very successful book of case studies entitled *Intuition on Demand*, published in 2006 and qualifications in management both internationally and nationally demonstrates she is well positioned to research, conceptualise and author this book: *Think Like an Entrepreneur – The Mindset of Success*.

This book will provide you with proven strategies and techniques to enable you to create the entrepreneurial venture you desire.

The connection between how entrepreneurs create successful businesses and how you can design your own entrepreneurial life, intentionally was not one that immediately entered my mind, at first.

Jane has easily seen that connection – another quality that intuitive entrepreneurs share – the ability to see opportunities holistically, making disparate patterns and connections work cohesively from a vast amount of information.

EMERITUS PROFESSOR MURRAY GILLIN

## Biography

### Emeritus Professor, Laurence Murray Gillin

Murray Gillin AM is Emeritus Professor of Entrepreneurship & Innovation at Swinburne University of Technology and Adjunct Professor at the University of Adelaide, S.A. During a career spanning over 50 years he worked in the fields of defence science and technology as an Engineer, Research Scientist and as Defence Research Attaché in the Australian Embassy Washington, USA; and in education as Dean of Engineering, Professor of Innovation and Entrepreneurship, Pro Vice-Chancellor (Industry/Academic Liaison) and Director Australian Graduate School of Entrepreneurship at Swinburne University of Technology.

# FOREWORD

He has special interests in wealth creation from engineering and innovation (is Past President of the Institution of Engineers, Australia), in work integrated learning (is Past-President of the World Association for Co-operative Education), and in entrepreneurship education and research (was Founding Chairman of the AGSE Entrepreneurship Research Conference 2004-2009).

In 2004, Murray was elected a Life Member of the BCERC Entrepreneurship Research Conference (USA), in 1994 was elected a Fellow of the Academy of Technological Sciences and Engineering and on Australia Day 1997, was awarded with an AM (Member of the Order of Australia) for his work in engineering, innovation and ongoing professional education.

Murray was the winner of the Inaugural 2001 Best Entrepreneurial Educator of the Year having founded Australia's and the World's first Masters Degree in Entrepreneurship and Innovation in 1989. In 1994, he initiated the development of the Institute for Innovation and Entrepreneurship as a viable commercial enterprise and joint venture between Swinburne University of Technology and Ernst & Young and created the AGSE Entrepreneurship Hall of Fame in 2006. Murray was a co-founder of the Pitcher Partners Institute for Entrepreneurship in partnership with ECIC. He is particularly interested in social and corporate entrepreneurship research and intuition in decision making.

# Research Questionnaire

 *Successful entrepreneurs are passionate, innovative risk-assessors whose actions are informed by accurate intuitions about future business opportunities.*

*Often this intuitive foreknowledge involves perception of implicit information about nonlocal objects and/or events by the body's psycho-physiological systems. A large body of experimental evidence has documented intuitive foreknowledge as a scientific fact, and recent studies using electro-physiological measures of autonomic nervous system activity have shown that such nonlocal intuition is related to the degree of emotional significance of the future event. Moreover, there is also solid experimental evidence that intentionally focused bio-emotional energy can have a subtle but significant (scientifically measurable) effect on nonlocal objects and events.*[i]

1. Have you ever experienced an intuition that has led to a breakthrough or new insight in your professional life?

2. Can you recall the exact circumstances leading up to that event? What happened as a result of the break-through – was it adopted or discarded? And if it was discarded, why?

---

[i] Bradley, Raymond Trevor, Institute for Whole Social Science, Institute of HeartMath®, California, USA, e-Motion Institute, Auckland, New Zealand; Murray Gillin, Australian Graduate School of Entrepreneurship; Dana Tomasino, Institute for Whole Social Science, e-Motion Institute. *Transformational Dynamics of Entrepreneurial Systems: The Organizational Basis of Intuitive Action*, Regional Frontiers of Entrepreneurial Research, 2008

3. Do you personally adopt practices such as meditation, relaxation, mindfulness to deliberately enable you to access breakthroughs or insights?

4. Have you experienced focusing your thought or intention to an event that has subsequently occurred in your life – if so please describe this scenario.

5. Do you consider yourself to be an intuitive or logical decision-maker in business or both?

6. In your opinion, how important is the role of intuition in the development of successful entrepreneurial ventures?

7. Anything else about intuition and intentionality that you would like to comment on?

# Acknowledgements

### The Interviewees

The interviews took place either face to face
or by phone / Skype over 2010 to 2014.

The interviewees' roles were current
at the time the interviews were conducted.

### Scientists

Emeritus Professor L Murray Gillin AM
Chairman, Ausentrepreneurs Sans Frontieres

Rollin Mc Craty
Executive Vice President and Director of Research,
HeartMath Institute®, USA

Emeritus Professor William A. Tiller, PhD
Chairman, The Tiller Foundation, USA

## Leading Thinkers

Michael Rennie
Director, McKinsey & Company Inc.

Tao de Haas
Psychotherapist, Expert Facilitator in Change, Corporate XL

John McFarlane
Chairman, Barclays Bank

Sonia Stanjovic
Principal, Pathways to Performance

## Entrepreneurs

Simon Bailey
Managing Director, Fulton Peak Pty Ltd
Strategist & Serial Entrepreneur

Simon Baker
Founder and CEO, Classified Ad Ventures
Serial Entrepreneur

Simon Cant
Co-Founder and Managing Director, Reinventure Group
Director, SocietyOne | Director, Nabo Australia
Serial Entrepreneur

Daniel Carlin
Founder, Elevate™ | Serial Entrepreneur

Evelyn Lundstrom
Founder, First Impressions Pty Ltd | Serial Entrepreneur

# Introduction

Entrepreneurs have an edge that people want to know more about. How do people adopt more entrepreneurial thinking? We know that entrepreneurs are passionate risk takers, focused individuals with a mantra of never give up! What is less known is their internal process to develop their personal mindset to perform at the highest level.

This book addresses the key issues of:

- What is the real 'secret' that successful entrepreneurs know and practise?
- How do breakthroughs and insights for ideas really occur?
- Are entrepreneurs born or made?
- Is it possible for entrepreneurial abilities to be enhanced?

We know from neuro-science that insights utilise different pathways in the brain than analysis. The analytical way of thinking continues to use existing brain circuitry that will never provide a breakthrough. Ninety-five per cent of our insights occur beyond the conscious mind. The conscious brain accounts for only five per cent of our brains cognitive functionality.[i] It cannot possibly absorb the increasing amount of information that we are faced with each day.

Creativity and imagination are declining due to multi-tasking and 24/7 connectivity. The speed of change and data overload requires

---
i  Lipton, Dr Bruce, PhD. *www.brucelipton.com*.

more adaptive, agile thinking. Data is not the whole story, what matters most is how we make sense of the data, and data insights will be generated through people.[ii] The world of work is changing, requiring the individual to be idea and knowledge-driven, less labour manually focused, as a direct result of disruptive technological change affecting every sector.

The latest scientific research reveals that the secret behind entrepreneurial success can be easily developed by everyone and is far beyond creative thinking, idea generation or brain-storming techniques.

Extensive research into what makes serial entrepreneurs successful led the author to the conclusion that entrepreneurial success is a combination of, or a formula of, choices that you make, **intentionally**. This formula is the road map for your entrepreneurial success.

This book contains the most valuable information on how to create your entrepreneurial success and achieve abundance in your professional and personal life ... in fact, anything you desire. 'Sounds too good to be 'true or 'it can't be that simple'... I can hear you saying!

Well it is both true and simple. I came across this astounding information in my work with Professor Murray Gillin, a scientist who has repeatedly observed and researched this formula being used by serial entrepreneurs in their businesses.

This formula might have continued to inhabit dusty academic shelves if it were not for a conversation Murray and I had one morning.

---

ii  Deloitte | AMP Capital. *"It's (almost) all about me. Workplace 2030: Built for us". July 2013*

## INTRODUCTION

How does an entrepreneur or team of entrepreneurs create a new business concept or innovation?

Ground-breaking research from the HeartMath Institute® in USA, in collaboration with Professor Murray Gillin's research, delivers an extraordinary answer, drawing extensively on an understanding of the human autonomic nervous system[iii] and quantum physics[iv].

*Think like an Entrepreneur – The Mindset of Success* demystifies and unpacks each aspect of this formula combined to allow you to create what you desire.

What makes this so strikingly different from every other book on the subject of how to create your entrepreneurial business is that the available books and programs detail one or more answers, **from an external view**. They focus on marketing, raising capital, targeting customers, building awareness – all very important elements for success.

**None have shown definitively how to create and design your business using a proven scientific framework and a formula of choices that you make intentionally.**

What I have done for you is to unbundle it … challenging each and every aspect of the formula, subjecting it to further research and many discussions; 'stress testing' it to the ultimate degree. The formula is designed to be used in sequence and the stages of each step in the

---

iii HeartMath Institute®. *www.heartmath.org*. "Human autonomic nervous system – the part of the nervous system that controls the body's internal functions, including heart rate, gastrointenstinal tract and secretions of many glands".

iv Encarta Dictionary. "Quantum physics – the theory describing behaviours and interactions of energy states which proposes that energy is subdivided into discrete amounts and that matter possesses wave properties".

formula are of utmost importance. As you work with the formula, you will become very skilled at moving rapidly through each stage.

The science of entrepreneurial success has been studied and pondered on by many thinkers in different arenas, from academics to scientists to anyone who has ever wondered if a formula exists. Many promise and few deliver, and the reason is simple. **They have discovered only one part of the formula and, just like a recipe for a wonderful soufflé, every ingredient and how you mix the ingredients determine the difference between a fluffy soufflé and one that does not rise!**

You may already be familiar with some components of the formula. What you will learn from this book is how to put it all together to achieve a successful outcome, every time.

The serial entrepreneurs who have been studied over many years have a consistent approach to setting up and generating a successful venture. This approach has been validated by research, time after time.

The interviews in this book demonstrate how the formula works and what can be achieved by its application combined with over 30 years of research. These findings long understood by the scientists and now validated with entrepreneurs, have never before been made available to the general public.

Each chapter is designed to be read independently, providing you with a step- by- step guide to each component of the formula. Within the chapters there are recommendations that you can apply immediately and a final practical technique ensuring your successful entrepreneurial life.

# INTRODUCTION

Other than that – there is no rulebook. Apply this formula to every aspect of your life and watch out! Your life will change radically, if that is your intention.

This book will challenge your thinking about how you can create and design your success, intentionally. Enjoy!

# CHAPTER 1
## The Science of Entrepreneurial Mindset

 *Entrepreneurs change the pattern of production by combining elements in new ways. They are, in this sense, innovators.*

JOSEPH A. SCHUMPETER, HARVARD PROFESSOR

The literal meaning of the word entrepreneur originated from the French verb 'entreprendre' which means 'to undertake'.

Entrepreneurs often foresee a new idea; develop a different way of thinking about a current product or service or adopt a radical position that disrupts their competitors' market. Entrepreneurs have an edge that people want to know more about.

How do people adopt entrepreneurial thinking? We want to experience new ideas, yet we do not fully understand the process by which real breakthroughs occur. How do we turn an idea into a viable business? All of the psychology and motivational material available has not successfully answered these critical questions, yet.

**Entrepreneurs have an ability that distinguishes them from others in business and the community. They have a heightened intuitive sense, leading them to uncover opportunities sometimes, previously unimagined.**

When I think about the late Steve Jobs, a true visionary and highly intuitive, the founder of Apple Computer, the company that revolutionised the personal computer and entertainment industry with their products, such as the *iMac*, *iPod*, *iPhone* and the *iPad*, I immediately recognise this entrepreneurial quality of heightened intuition.

Steve was a great fan of intuition. In his commencement speech to the graduating students at Stanford University in 2005, he spoke about intuition and passion as the two most important aspects of building a successful business. His powerful speech to the graduates truly reflected an unorthodox life defined by following both his intuition and his heart.

Here is an excerpt as he outlined his decision to leave an expensive college education. The full transcript and video can be viewed at: http://news.stanford.edu/news/2005/june15/jobs-061505.html.

*So I decided to drop out and trust that it would all work out OK. It was pretty scary at the time, but looking back it was one of the best decisions I ever made. The minute I dropped out I could stop taking the required classes that didn't interest me, and begin dropping in on the ones that looked interesting.*

*It wasn't all romantic. I didn't have a dorm room, so I slept on the floor in friends' rooms, I returned coke bottles for the 5¢ deposits to buy food with, and I would walk the 7 miles across town every Sunday night to get one good meal a week at the Hare Krishna temple. I loved it. And much of what I stumbled into by following my curiosity and intuition turned out to be priceless later on. Let me give you one example:*

*Reed College at that time offered perhaps the best calligraphy instruction in the country. Throughout the campus every poster, every label on every drawer was beautifully hand calligraphed. Because I had dropped out and didn't have to take the normal classes, I decided to take a calligraphy class to learn how to do this. I learned about serif and san serif typefaces, about varying the amount of space between different letter combinations, about what makes great typography great. It was beautiful, historical, artistically subtle in a way that science can't capture, and I found it fascinating.*

*None of this had even a hope of any practical application in my life. But ten years later, when we were designing the first Macintosh computer, it all came back to me. And we designed it all into the Mac. It was the first computer with beautiful typography. If I had never dropped in on that single course in college, the Mac would have never had multiple typefaces or proportionally spaced fonts. And since Windows just copied the Mac, it's likely that no personal computer would have them. If I had never dropped out, I would have never dropped in on this calligraphy class, and personal computers might not have the wonderful typography that they do. Of course it was impossible to connect the dots looking forward when I was in college. But it was very, very clear looking backwards ten years later.*

*Again, you can't connect the dots looking forward; you can only connect them looking backwards. So you have to trust that the dots will somehow connect in your future.*

***You have to trust in something – your gut, destiny, life, karma, whatever. This approach has never let me down, and it has made all the difference in my life.***

As the Apple Computer business grew, Steve found himself in 1984 being dismissed as CEO by the Managing Director he had hired, John Sculley and the Board. He then founded an entirely new business called NEXT Software, subsequently selling it to Apple and developed many products responsible for Apples' dominance in the entertainment market today.

Steve went onto talk about the importance of passion: loving what you do:

*I'm pretty sure none of this would have happened if I hadn't been fired from Apple. It was awful tasting medicine, but I guess the patient needed it. Sometimes life hits you in the head with a brick. Don't lose faith. I'm convinced that the only thing that kept me going was that I loved what I did. You've got to find what you love. And that is as true for your work as it is for your lovers. Your work is going to fill a large part of your life, and the only way to be truly satisfied is to do what you believe is great work. And the only way to do great work is to love what you do. If you haven't found it yet, keep looking. Don't settle. As with all matters of the heart, you'll know when you find it. And, like any great relationship, it just gets better and better as the years roll on. So keep looking until you find it. Don't settle.*

And I wondered did Steve know just how successful his passion to follow his heart would make him personally and professionally.

Steve re-iterated his key message to the students:

*Your time is limited, so don't waste it living someone else's life. Don't be trapped by dogma – which is living with the results of other people's thinking.*

***Don't let the noise of others' opinions drown out your own inner voice. And most important, have the courage to follow your heart and intuition****. They somehow already know what you truly want to become. Everything else is secondary.*

## The first step for an entrepreneurial business occurs from a strong intuition that propels the idea or opportunity into being.

I often wondered just how much intuition played in the development of successful entrepreneurial business. I knew in my heart that intuition was a powerful guiding force in my own life. I realised that when I had ignored its [intuition] subtle often persistent messages, I had later regretted my choices. For the past 17 years, I have worked as an intuitive consultant, training and coaching business executives to utilise more of their intuitive intelligence in decision-making.

I am often asked what is intuition, really is. Intuition can be broadly defined as *direct knowing*. A sense of inner certainty 'I just know'. How often have you had this experience? When I ask people this question, I have always received a positive response. Where much confusion lies, however is in the numerous definitions of intuition. It is often defined by the individual's physiological experience of intuition: *I had a feeling, I just knew, I trusted my gut*. Many people relate their experiences of ignoring their intuition, and later regretting it.

Intuition has been described as an inner knowing, an awareness, a gut feeling, an inspiration, a revelation. That niggling feeling, the dream or the sudden insight, 'Aha' moment, the Eureka factor, that hunch which led you to a new discovery or a different way of looking at a situation or a person, a certain knowing, a sense of things not being quite correct, that is your intuition!

What intuitive moments have you experienced? Have you had a feeling about a person, perhaps an instant dislike, whom you met at work or in a social situation -and later discovered that your feeling was justified?

The word 'intuition' comes from a Latin word, 'intueri,' meaning to 'look within'. The Macquarie dictionary defines intuition as 'the direct perception of truths, facts independently of any reasoning process'.

Intuition is often misrepresented by other words in our daily life. When you hear someone speak of 'instinct', they are probably referring to 'intuition'. Instinct is dependent on an external event whereas intuition always appears from an internal focus.

Here is my definition developed after years of research into this fascinating field:

*Intuition is your internal database of knowledge and experience blended with your brain's conscious and unconscious pattern recognition skills. Intuition is an essential part of your intelligence.*

*Intuitive knowing is a process by which nonlocal information, normally outside of the range of conscious awareness, is immediately sensed and perceived by the body's psycho-physiological systems.*

Why is intuition important? Decision-making is not solely rational! It is influenced by both the context of the decision and our emotional state. Daniel Goleman in his book 'Emotional Intelligence' reported that 66% of senior CEO's and managers of corporations in the USA acknowledge they use, gut-feel, intuition, or a sense in making critical decisions.

Ninety-five per cent of our awareness is beyond the conscious mind and, as you will read later in this book, the subconscious mind drives our behaviours. Our behaviours are a result of beliefs, values, education, our environment and societal norms which are then filtered by our view of the world in which we live and our subsequent behaviours occur as a result.

In increasingly complex and ambiguous environments, intuitive styles of decision-making rule. In critical care situations, medical professionals, emergency workers such as fire fighters, army personnel and law enforcement officials learn how to trust their intuition. It is regarded as an essential competency at work.

Our education system has successfully attempted to destroy intuition. In the past 40 years, the skills valued in our Western society have been dominated by the factual, analytical and practical intelligences. Our reliance on logical thinking emerged as we began to trust the words of others more than our own 'inner knowing'. Society now dictates an almost exclusive reliance on a mode of thinking that is clearly not serving our current needs. Research suggests that up to 50 per cent of decisions made with analysis are later proven to be incorrect.

Scientists readily admit that when they first test a hypothesis, it emerges from a vague idea or intuition about a set of circumstances which they then proceed to test by logical measures. In today's society, with little time for analysis and ever- increasing pressure to make accurate decisions under stress, intuition is an invaluable skill easily available to everyone.

Everyone is intuitive. You already have had intuitive experiences. It is your choice whether to take notice and act on your intuition. It is your own internal guidance system available to you at all times. Just like a computer's hard drive, it is always alert, waiting for recognition.

Your intuitive intelligence is a skill that you can develop intentionally, just like a set of muscles. Intuition tells you what to do, not what not to do.

It is characterised by positive messages. Sometimes we ignore the messages, always I believe, to our detriment. When you acknowledge and work with your intuition, you will have a reliable ally. Your intuition will continue to alert you to possible outcomes, even when you ignore it. Working with your intuition starts when you discover your own unique intuitive response and have the confidence to trust in and act on it.

Often fear intervenes in our decision-making process. Fear of standing out from the crowd, fear of making a decision that may later be proven wrong, fear of admitting that intuition was the source of your decision. These are some of the major barriers to making choices that include your intuitive mind.

Your intuition is characterised by a deep resonance and certainty. Many people who live in stressed, pressurised environments have become unbalanced and have lost touch with their innate wisdom. You will become more aware and trusting of your inner self as you begin to shift the balance from reliance on your external environment to your internal guidance. Using your intuitive mind is just like exercising a muscle – the more you use it the more its potency improves, just like your tennis or golf game. Intuition often appears to us in different ways – it does not take the same route as logical information. It is elusive, often contrary to the analysis. Sometimes it encourages us to radically change our actions. When there is an increasing amount of information, and few precedents exist, you may have little choice except to rely on intuition. When this strategy works, often we dismiss the outcome as a fortuitous on- off event.

## How does your intuition communicate to you?

Discovering your dominant intuitive response is the first step. Intuitive responses can present themselves in different forms. For example, you may get an intuitive flash (visual image) images, pictures or you may hear a voice (auditory) some people hear words or phrases. You may have a 'gut' feeling (kinaesthetic) which is a strong physical sensation or an emotional feeling about an issue or person. All of these methods of receiving intuitive information are valid. People experience intuition in different ways.

People who rely on intuition in their everyday life or work don't think about where it comes from. For other people, dreams are a viable method of receiving intuition about all aspects of their life. Some people have a single dominant sensory based response; a client sensed a distinctive odour every time her intuition wanted to alert her to information about a person or situation. This odour was dramatically different to any other she had ever experienced!

How many times have you said to yourself "I knew that" and "I wish I had followed my intuition"! Many people have had this experience yet we do not always listen to our intuitive mind. This illustrates that our intuitive mind is very active, often in retrospect. The willingness to listen and act on your intuition requires trust and confidence.

Intuition can be perceived whether or not you have previous knowledge about a situation/person or event. Intuitive knowing with precedent is somewhat easier for most of us to accept compared to intuitive knowledge without precedent. However, both types fit into definitions of intuition – knowledge that is not invoked from the logical mind. Intuition is developed through sensory awareness. However, the willingness to listen to your inner self requires a level of self-confidence and self-esteem.

I discovered that the people, who value intuition as a reliable ally in decision-making, often viewed it as a 'secret weapon'. I noticed that intuition was mentioned in the material on creating an entrepreneurial business, only receiving scant attention.

As an author and researcher on all matters related to intuition, I regularly review media publications and websites to find out who is doing what – some people call it "competitive intelligence". A friend spied a magazine in a book store with a cover story on entrepreneurship and intuition featuring the research of Professor Murray Gillin. She immediately said "I think you should contact this fellow".

I arranged a meeting with Murray at the university campus where he was directing the Australian Graduate School of Entrepreneurship in Melbourne, Australia. Reading about Murray in advance of the meeting was staggeringly impressive. His career spanned several decades in senior level positions in defence research and development as an Attaché in Washington, and conducting ground breaking research on entrepreneurship. Murray assessed one of the first incubators to generate new ideas and innovative businesses in Cambridge, England, traditionally a 'non-business outcome' university town. This look alike 'Silicon Valley' delivered to the UK economy in excess of seven billion pounds in GDP in one year, directly attributable to converting the power of knowledge into real wealth.

With this array of impressive credentials, I was not sure what to expect and felt honoured that he had agreed to spend some time with me that day discussing intuition, a topic I have always been passionately drawn to research.

A short man with a welcoming smile and firm handshake met me at the student cafeteria in the university grounds. With a huge degree of modesty and infinite patience, he answered all my questions and raised many more that morning in our discussion. Murray was frustrated with the psychological view of intuition as pure pattern recognition from retrieval of deep memory being based in and from the brain.

Becoming quite excited, he had debated this viewpoint vigorously many times and felt at odds with the academics who were his peers. Somewhat damningly, he spoke of the academic world as a group who resist exploring concepts that appear outside conventional understanding. Murray went on to liken these academics to thinkers in earlier centuries who refused to acknowledge that the world was indeed not flat! The role of science Murray stated was to challenge and make new discoveries, not to just accept the established view. This is Murray's daily mantra.

Entrepreneurship was to become a later interest and a significant passion, Murray confided to me. His research in entrepreneurship led him to examine intuition.

Murray had consistently observed that 'serial' or 'repeat' entrepreneurs had adopted intuitive knowledge to create successful businesses. During this time, he developed and delivered the first ever Masters of Entrepreneurship and Innovation. Since 1989, this program has been successfully delivered internationally to thousands of graduates.

In his capacity in the academic world, Murray continues to deliver, write, research and consult to a wide range of students and businesses in Australia, South East Asia, Europe and USA. He has formed a new group of savvy entrepreneurs which he has designated Ausentreprenurs sans Frontieres or Australian entrepreneurs without borders. The aim of this unique program is to use graduates from entrepreneurial education programs to provide the resources and knowledge they have gained from their education to build selected micro-financed start-ups in developing nations into growth ventures that deliver real wealth to their communities.

An entrepreneur creates successful new business concepts or opportunities – easily.

The first step is always the intuition for an idea or opportunity, according to Murray's research. He researched the exact role that intuition played in entrepreneurial decision-making.

Murray's definition of intuition was different from the psychological viewpoint. He views intuition as beyond the brain. Murray defined the experience of intuition as not confined to cognitive perception; it involves the entire psycho-physiological system, often manifesting through a wide range of emotional feelings and physiological changes experienced throughout the body. This whole-body intuition can and has been measured.

This is ground breaking. Intuitive abilities can be trained and strengthened, just like a set of muscles. Entrepreneurial intuition can be improved enabling entrepreneurs to create new business opportunities and enhance their existing business. We are increasing dependent on a knowledge-based economy as we move away from more task based occupations. This research and its findings demonstrate how we can create and sustain new thinking to develop more divergent business opportunities.

I discussed the role that intuition plays in the development of successful new ventures extensively with Professor Gillin. Surprisingly, only a limited amount of data has been researched on the attributes that define successful entrepreneurs, most research has focused on individual characteristics such as motivation, 'thinking outside the square' and their persistence. Murray wanted to delve more deeply, to discover the essence of what makes an entrepreneur successful, beyond the obvious measures.

I asked Murray how he conducted his research:

*In 1988 I had developed the Entrepreneurship and Innovation Masters program – a world first – at Swinburne University of Technology in Melbourne, Victoria. I was interested in what made entrepreneurs different in terms of their capacity to make decisions.*

*We all know that entrepreneurs, typically serial entrepreneurs, use other means to make decisions; means other than analysis. Text books, business promoters, academics all focus on the role of analysis in the decision-making process, and analysis is important, analysis is necessary but successful entrepreneurs don't make their decisions on analysis alone.*

They make decisions based on feelings, other experiences, and that's what we're trying to understand. We're trying to understand how successful entrepreneurs go about making decisions, and learn from the process so that it may be taught.

Initially, we organised a series of interviews with serial entrepreneurs at the Cambridge Technopol. The Cambridge Technopol is an exciting place. Up until 1980, Cambridge University focused on knowledge generation and Cambridge, the city, was a sleepy; very much a market town. There were only about 50 high tech companies with around about 2,000 employees. That's it. In what indeed is one of the world's best universities, with terrific new knowledge being created all the time, there was no commercialisation. No entrepreneurial exploitation. Anyway, years later, they have 3,500 high tech businesses, which are related to the university and its network, employing 50,000 people.

What's really interesting is the contribution to the GDP of the UK this precinct creates – approximately GBP 7.6 billion. That's a tremendous transition.

The important thing is that the area has also become a breeding ground for successful 'serial' entrepreneurs. So, we started to interview a number of these very successful entrepreneurs. In the interviews, we wanted them to tell us what affected their decision-making. We recorded the interviews and transcribed them. We then analysed the content, and what came back, loud and clear, was that the entrepreneurs said that their decisions were influenced by feelings.

They said, 'Yes', we use analysis, but when we make decisions, we often have a gut feel, an instinct, some sense of intuition.' These were the sorts of words that were used, again and again. So we said, 'Ah-ha! There is something happening here.'

Returning to intuition and its role in serial entrepreneurial behaviour, Murray continued:

*The HeartMath Institute® and my research concluded that our intuition is a unique form of sensory perception that is connected to and constantly communicating with the universal field of energy. Some scientists believe that the brain is simply a sophisticated retrieval mechanism, accessing all information that is held in the quantum field. You may like to think of it as a giant database.*

*To test subjects [intuitive preference], we used certain protocols, on a computer. We begin with a simulated roulette wheel, where the subjects make a betting decision. While they're making that decision, before they have all the information they need to make a decision, we were measuring their heart rate and skin conductance, monitoring their Autonomic Nervous System [the part of the nervous system in humans and other vertebrates that controls involuntary activity such as the action of the heart and glands, breathing, digestive processes, and reflex action]*

*Then we turn to business cases. We used something like fifty cases, all high growth businesses. I separated SMEs [small medium enterprises] from entrepreneurial businesses on the basis of growth. Twenty-five are case studies of successful growth companies. Twenty-five are companies that have failed. We present the subjects with very limited data on the industry, the way the project is being funded, the structure of the enterprise, who owns it, that type of thing. We give them $ A100,000 to invest in the case studies they believe will be high growth.*

*Of course, they are also using their cognitive decision-making processes. There is no question of that. I watched them, and if they know the industry well, they are more likely to be decisive. What we're doing, is measuring what's happening just prior to that point. We measured these effects and what we found was there was a level of significance in their capacity to choose what was the correct answer, over the wrong answer.*

*The findings were significantly better than what you would expect with just a roulette experiment, above chance. What we found is that there is a correlation between pre-stimulus behaviour and a response. For example, the heart rate [variability] changes, it decelerates, before a subject makes a correct/incorrect decision. What we were measuring was heart rate variability and skin conductance and we could show without doubt that the person was starting to form how they were going to respond some four to six seconds before the brain came in to act – before any cognitive activity.[i]*

*Now, I am talking about trends. The whole purpose is that if we can understand what makes intuition effective then we can design interventions to enhance the capacity of the individual to improve their decision-making performance.*

Are you suggesting that entrepreneurs have a greater propensity than other people for making decisions using methods other than analysis, I asked Murray?

*I'm not arguing that entrepreneurs are the only people who use intuition. The reason I decided to study serial entrepreneurs was quite deliberate, because serial entrepreneurs have started several successful businesses. This eliminates the argument that their success is based on luck. And they freely acknowledge that there is something that they rely on, which is not just analysis. I'm certainly not the first*

---

i  HeartMath Institute® , The Science of the Heart. www.heartmath.org.

*to look at the role of intuition in business decision-making. They only look at cognitive intuition.*

*We're certainly the first to look at what you might call an electro-physiological explanation for components of intuition. I have to keep emphasising that what we're looking at is not just intuition, because intuition does, in fact, take into account what happens in the brain and the process of cognitive analysis.*

*Intuitive decision-making is informing entrepreneurs' subsequent choices.*

This research of serial entrepreneurs is a world first and has since been published in numerous leading academic journals globally and presented at Entrepreneurial conferences. The initial study has been replicated using the same testing protocols at the University of Tehran in 2010. This study further corroborated the initial findings from Bradley et al (2010) that electrophysiological measures can detect nonlocal intuition in repeat entrepreneurs. This research was conducted amongst a group of repeat entrepreneurs in Iran, adding a different context culturally for evaluation of the initial research. The results offered new evidence on the amplification of the nonlocal intuition signal by socio-physiological fields. And it demonstrated that the entrepreneurs' ability to detect the intuitive foresight was not related to personal characteristics of age, education level, business experience or size of organisation.

How does an entrepreneur first perceive an opportunity for a new enterprise? The next chapter will look at the second step to deliberately generate opportunities for success – by easily accessing the field of opportunity.

## KEY POINTS

- Intuition is always present, whether you acknowledge it or not.
- Many people ignore their intuition to later regret their choices.
- Intuition communicates with you in different ways.
- Isolating your dominant response is the key to becoming more in touch with it.
- Successful entrepreneurs trust and act on their intuition, to establish the business vision or initial idea.
- Intuitive decision-making is informing entrepreneurs' subsequent choices and this intuitive action can be measured using electro-physiological tools.

# CHAPTER 2
## The Frequency of Opportunity

 *Everything is energy and that is all there is to it. Match the frequency of the reality you want and you cannot help but get that reality. It can be no other way. This is not philosophy, this is physics.*

ALBERT EINSTEIN

How an entrepreneur thinks and feels is a critical aspect of how they create successful businesses. We know from the previous chapter that entrepreneurs have great intuition. Your intuition is an energy that carries a resonance, or a frequency which is as unique to you, as your own set of fingerprints. Every thought, word and action carries its own energetic frequency. Your frequency level determines how you communicate, energetically with the world you live in. When you have positive thoughts, you resonate at a higher frequency. When you have negative thoughts, your frequency becomes lowered or depressed. This affects every aspect of your life, from your career to your health. This ground-breaking discovery has huge significance for the way we think and behave.

Albert Einstein, created the now famous equation e=mc² in 1905 named the Theory of Relativity. His intuitive moment led him to the conclusion that mass is equal to energy. The rest of the equation represents the speed of light to measure how much energy a given mass represents.

Energy is made up of atoms and molecules broken down into waves (energy) and particles (physical matter) that have the same qualities. Nothing is solid, purely energy or frequency patterns of information allowing human beings to affect their environment at a sub-atomic level.

Everything is interconnected, in a unified field of information that is available to all, through the concept of nonlocality. A state of coherence created by positive emotions allows access to this quantum field. The stronger our passionate attention with an aligned state of coherence opens up the sea of probabilities. We do create our reality by attuning our **thoughts and emotions**, consciously and unconsciously, to whatever we desire or fear.

Recent research in psychology, biology, and neurophysiology suggests that human beings are, indeed, quantum beings. Even though a person may be viewed primarily as a material being, there is also an invisible, non-material dimension (mind, consciousness or spirit) whose functioning appears to be affected by quantum principles.[i] The word 'quantum' was introduced early in the 20th century to describe the physics of the subatomic realm. The subatomic realm refers to everything in the physical world that is smaller than an atom. The word quantum literally means "a quantity of something". Quantum field theory in physics is defined as the interaction of two separate physical

---

[i] Shelton, Charlotte K and Darling, John R, *The quantum skills model in management: a new paradigm to enhance effective leadership*, School of Management, Rockhurst University, Kansas City, Missouri, USA.

systems, as particles and is attributed to a field that extends from one to the other and is manifested in a particle exchange between the two systems.

Quantum physics is, therefore, the study of subatomic particles in motion (Shelton, Quantum Leaps, 1999, 1-4). However, subatomic particles are not material things; rather, they are probability tendencies – **energy with potentiality**.

A state of coherence is created by positive emotions and slowing down our brainwave patterns does allow access to the quantum field. The power of visualisation with feeling positive of already achieving your desire, with clarity and consistency, will strengthen the electromagnetic signal that pulls you to a potential reality of what you want.

If you can imagine an event occurring in your life based on a desire, that reality already exists as a potential in the quantum field. When you change your electromagnetic signature to match one of the potentials in the field, you will be drawn to it or it will find you in your new reality.

In his research Professor Murray Gillin, discovered that entrepreneurs could easily attune to this quantum 'field of opportunity' or potentiality. Murray commented on this when he said:

*What I found was that these [serial] entrepreneurs had a propensity for intuition and intentionality. And that's where we're picking up the evidence that the Autonomic Nervous System is actually collecting information from the quantum, from the surrounding environment, and then feeding that information up to the brain. Even more startling, we found that entrepreneurs are able to receive information from nonlocal sources about a future event – 6 to 7 seconds before the event actually happens. We discovered this by analysis of skin conductance and heart rate variability systems. We started to recognise that what is in the [quantum] Field is already there and hence this input to the issue of passionate concentration, then means you then receive the information.*

## Intuitive decision-making is informing entrepreneurs' subsequent choices.

This principle of nonlocality is a key differentiator in Murray's research on intuition.

Murray explained further:

*Intuition is not confined simply to cognitive-based perception, but involves the entire psycho-physiological system often associated with emotional and or physiological responses (McCraty et al., 2004a; Bierman, 2000; Radin, 1997a; Spottiswoode and May, 2003). Intuition, as it is currently defined, is based upon very linear understandings of cognition in processing information already existent in the data banks of the brain. However, using the example of physics, and the fact that humans are also composed of energy fields and potentials, it follows that these fields can interact with others in the universe.*

*In other words, the human is interconnected to the environment. It is a process by which information normally outside of the conscious processes is sensed and perceived in the body and mind as certainty of knowledge or feeling about an occurrence that is yet to happen.*

*We believe that such intuition (nonlocal) involves the body's connection to a field of energy beyond normal consciousness (Spottiswoode and May, 2003; Loye, 1983). This has been referred to as interconnectedness or collective consciousness.*

*Nonlocal intuition can then be examined as that active information available from the surrounding quantum field (that is 'outside' the body) and its interaction with the energy particles of the human body.*

The HeartMath Institute®, founded in 1991, by Doc Childre have been studying the relationship between the human heart and the brain and the way in which this relationship affects physical, mental and emotional health and human performance.

*There is a brain in the heart, metaphorically speaking," says Dr Rollin McCraty of the HeartMath Institute®. "The heart contains neurons and ganglia that have the same function as those of the brain, such as memory. It's an anatomical fact," he said. "What people don't know that well is that the heart actually sends more information to the brain [than the brain does to the heart]," he added.*

According to Harvard Medical School, chemical 'conversations' between the heart and the brain affect both organs. Depression, stress, loneliness, a positive outlook, and other psycho-social factors influence the heart. The health of the heart can also affect the brain and the mind.

Work conducted at the HeartMath Institute® Research Centre, by McCraty, Atkinson and Bradley has confirmed that there are instances when 'intuitive insights' are unrelated to information and experiences stored in the subconscious further confirming that intuition is beyond the brain.

The heart's intelligence through its electro-magnetic field is communicating with the universal energy field, scanning its so called database for potential opportunities.

**Entrepreneurs easily access this field of potential opportunities.**

Furthermore, it has been shown that entrepreneurs working together share an attitudinal bond that enables their joint attunement to this field of knowledge. This groundbreaking research demonstrates that we operate in a collective environment and our thinking directly influences every individual in the world.

Continuing my conversation with Murray, I asked, "So the body is connected somehow to a Field. Please explain exactly how this works."

*It may help if we talk for a moment about quantum physics. We know that there is a collective energetic field that surrounds all of us. It surrounds animals and plants, too. In my view it is connected to the Source of all that is: God, if you like. In experiments with Kirilian photography, this energetic field can be easily seen. If you think about the historical paintings or religious images of saints or so-called holy people, an aura or halo is always depicted around the head and shoulders of the person. After all, we are all energy. When you break it right down, atoms, molecules, particles, sub-particles – all that exists- is energy. Einstein and many other scientists since agree that energy lives on, it never dies. We have become immune to seeing this energy field today without the use of specialised equipment.*

*This type of sensing is not unique to humans. Throughout recorded history, accurate premonitions of impending natural disasters by birds and animals have been recorded. A comprehensive study of animal's premonition concluded that pets can sense the return of their owners long before they can see or hear them (Sheldrake, 1999; McCraty et al., 2004b).*

This type of thinking may be a radical concept for many people to accept, however it is the basis of how entrepreneurs actually access and communicate with the quantum field.

Murray quoted directly from his research with HeartMath Institute®:

*"It is their bio-emotional attunement to an order of energetically encoded quantum holographic information beyond space/time that provides access to the rationality of implicit potentials and that sets them apart from other business actors. In short, attunement to this energetic domain of quantum holographic information in-forms (gives shape to) creativity and entrepreneurship: it is the means by which future opportunities can be intuitively located and intentionally actualized into being".* [ii]

When I first heard the above paragraph, I thought, in some way this is not dissimilar to so called 'New Age' writing the idea that thought creates reality... or is it that the new agers had it right the first time?

I paused to reflect before asking Murray for more clarification: Are you saying that it is possible for a person to access exactly what they desire by engaging their intuition and attuning to the opportunity that is available in the quantum field? This seems too simple.

Murray replied:

*Remember what we talked about earlier. The heart is one of the greatest resonators in the body, communicating easily through the*

---

[ii] Gillin, Murray; LaPira, Frank; McCraty, Rollin; Bradley, Raymond Trevor. "Before Cognition: The Active Contribution of the Heart / ANS to Intuitive Decision Making as measured on Repeat Entrepreneurs in the Cambridge Technopol". HeartMath Institute®.

*Autonomic Nervous System, [functions of the nervous system that are controlled without your conscious knowledge, for example your heartbeat], both sending and receiving information without your conscious awareness.*

*The HeartMath Institute® discovered that communication between the heart and brain is actually a dynamic, ongoing, two-way dialogue, with each organ continuously influencing the other's function. The heart communicates with the brain in four major ways: neurologically (through the transmission of nerve impulses), biochemically (via hormones and neurotransmitters), biophysically (through pressure waves) and energetically (through electromagnetic field interactions).[iii]*

Murray had discovered that entrepreneurial success is dependent upon acting on your intuition, having a passionate desire for the idea or opportunity and intentionally making choices to create the outcome.

**We know that the more an entrepreneur maintains coherent attention to the subject of interest [the opportunity], the greater the level of intuitive foreknowledge.**

What exactly do you mean when you talk about coherent attention, I asked Murray.

*Coherence, in this context means when the body systems and sub-systems are in harmony. This can be shown in the heart rate variability studies.*

*A coherent heart is one that has smooth, ordered heart-rhythm patterns that can be seen on an electrocardiogram. This is not heart*

---

[iii] HeartMath Institute®, "The Science of the Heart". *www.heartmath.org*

*beat – this is the heart rhythm or beat to beat variability. When heart rhythm patterns are coherent, the ability to sense intuitive information is heightened. An incoherent heart is marked by jagged, disordered or irregular heart rhythm patterns. And it has been shown to have lowered sensitivity to perceiving intuitive information.*

*Think about it this way, you can generate a coherent heart rhythm just by feeling appreciation, compassion, love and caring – these feelings are converted into coherent heart rhythm patterns and are sent to the brain which searches for an appropriate response learnt from previous similar situations.*

It has been shown that people experiencing coherent heart rhythms have more Alpha brain wave patterns – slowing down their brain waves to between 8-12 Hz per second. Measuring this real-time feedback with technologies developed by the HeartMath Institute® enables you to manage your levels of stress, emotions and intuition more effectively.

The following graphs from one of the HeartMath Institute® tools demonstrate the difference in heart rate variability from a person who is in a frustrated emotional state to one who is experiencing an appreciative emotional state.

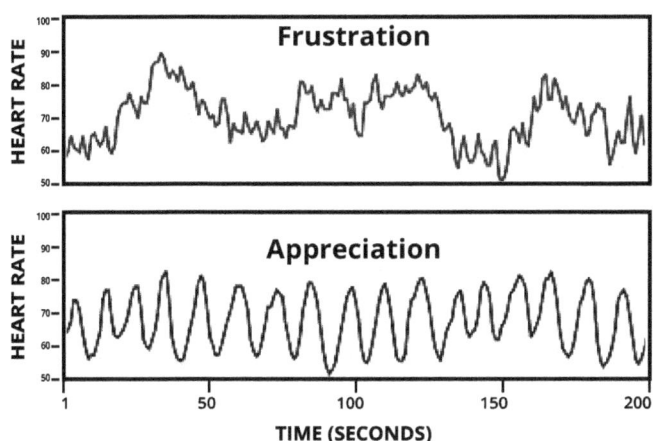

We can measure effectively with this unique tool, not just individual coherence – a whole team or group of people.

At Murray's instigation, I contacted Rollin McCraty, Ph.D., Executive Vice President and Director of Research at HeartMath Institute® to learn more about their research and application of coherence models in their training programs. He and his research team regularly participate in collaborative studies with other U.S. and international scientific, medical and educational institutions. McCraty is an internationally recognised authority on heart-rate variability, heart-rhythm coherence and the effects of positive and negative emotions on human psychophysiology. He is widely published in those and other research areas. I asked Rollin, who is using these techniques and why:

> *The Armed forces have had a lot of success – we have contracts with the Navy and the Air Force. They have a much perceived need to maintain composure and sustain resilience in these high tempo, high stressful contexts. The other place that there is a lot of traction is in hospitals. Primarily for hospital staff and that's usually an ROI [return on investment] associated. We used healthcare costs, we use absenteeism and [staff] turnover so multiple studies over a long time period have now achieved millions of dollars of savings to the hospital after they incorporated HeartMath training to their staff.*

**When you create your electro-magnetic signature to match one of the potentials in the Field, you will be drawn to it or it will find you in your new reality.**

The language of the Field is one of coherent emotion. When you are incoherent, the messages/signals are confused. Coherence produces chemical changes in the body and the brain. Intention is the key that unlocks everything that you desire – belief in the outcome is not enough. Create a 'positive' state of intention – purposefully put yourself in a state of intentionality with clarity and coherence and visualise your desired outcome. Going beyond fear and the physical mind to access information from the Field opens up opportunities and new knowledge of all that exists as a potentiality.

Fear paralyses us by the release of powerful chemicals and hormones on brain cell receptor sites which link to other cell receptor sites. Nerve cells that fire together, wire together.

To break free of old patterns and to see the whole picture demands a new way of thinking. If we are locked into the old, we stay locked in. When we are locked into the old patterns, possibilities become limited by pre-conceived beliefs, values, past experiences and education.

Breakthroughs occur beyond possibilities by consciously creating an intuition, having positive emotion, passionate attention, intentionally aligning to the field to bring the creation to reality.

So logically the more that you maintain a coherent heart rhythm, not only are you more in touch with intuition, you are re-programming your brain to respond in more loving, compassionate and positive way to any situation you may face.

Neuro-science informs us that the brain is changed by every new experience that we have. I had been reading a lot of neuroscience and the facts about neuro-plasticity – the ability we have to re-formulate our brain – and therefore our behaviour, what an exciting idea!

Yet I began to wonder, what is it that gets in the way of creating what it is that which we desire? If we knew that it is just a matter of clearly attuning our desire to a vibrationary level… or is it that we are unclear and sending out mixed messages.

What gets in the way? The next chapter will delve into one of the barriers to success … and explains why it is easier for some people to achieve what they desire.

## KEY POINTS

- When you create your electro-magnetic signature to match one of the potentials in the Field, you will be drawn to it or it will find you in your new reality.
- When you access your intuitive intelligence, having passionate intention to achieve the object of desire and attune to the energetic field from a coherent, heart based state you will bring to you what you desire.
- You can easily attune to a coherent state by altering your thinking to become more positive.
- Intuition is the first step: opening the doorway to your desires
- Passion and intention – the second and third steps is to become what it is that you desire.
- Attunement to the energetic field provides more information and permits coherence to the opportunity.

# CHAPTER 3

## The Power of Beliefs

 *The map is not the territory ...*

KORZYBSKI

What gets in the way of creating your successful new business venture?

There are numerous factors that can hinder or block your progress in developing entrepreneurial thinking. Did you know that 95 per cent of all human behaviours emanate from the sub-conscious mind, beyond your conscious awareness? Personal behaviours are driven by many factors such as beliefs, values, assumptions, expectations, conditioning, and your experiences or personal history. Add to these behaviours your desires, intentions and emotions and you have a potent force for creation or destruction!

To review what impact these factors can have on individual behaviours could fill many books. Let's examine one of the most important factors in detail: beliefs.

Beliefs are defined as an acceptance by the mind that something is true or real, often underpinned by an emotional or spiritual sense of certainty. They can also be defined as a statement, principle or doctrine that a person or group accepts as truth for him or herself about a personal or world viewpoint.

Where do our beliefs originate? I took this question to eminent psychotherapist and human potential specialist, Tao de Haas. Tao, a Dutchman came to Australia over 40 years ago and after a business career re-educated himself to study the workings of the human being. Beyond his bright blue eyes, his boyish good looks and his still slight Dutch accent when he expresses certain words, lies a individual who is passionate about discovering and working with the human-ness of the tens of thousands of people that he has coached and trained to help them benefit from a deeper understanding of themselves and consequently, other people.

I asked Tao, "What have you observed about the people you have worked with that have become successful entrepreneurs."

Tao answered, somewhat enigmatically:

*Why is it that some people do exactly the same thing that somebody else does and it works for one person and not for the other?*

*I think there's a huge element of luck involved. You and I have talked about the metaphor of two people building a beautiful identical kite. One kite will catch the wind and the other does not catch any wind.*

*First, you need to have a certain amount of talent or ambition or courage, the second one is unbelievable amount of hard work and determination, then the Goddess Futuna – Lady Luck – [will] either kiss you or bless you, or not.*

# THE POWER OF BELIEFS

I countered to Tao, that, "there are many other factors as well, for example, your beliefs, could he explain what impact your beliefs have?"

*Belief systems are important. As Henry Ford said: whether you think you can or you think you can't, you're right! Beliefs are a vital ingredient in determining if you are successful or not. It would be most unlikely to be successful, if you believe that you cannot be. I sometimes say that you need to make it possible for the Goddess Fortuna to be able to come and support you. Beliefs that are aligned with what you want to achieve are the invitation for her to do so. I mean this metaphorically of course.*

Do beliefs influence your success so strongly, I asked Tao.

*Think about it this way: the sum total of your beliefs forms 'your story'. The stories you create help you make sense of your life and the world you live in. This influences every aspect of your life. Creating stories happens automatically and without them, you would not be able to make sense of yourself or the world around you. The 'quality' of your story hugely influences how you live your life and the feedback that you get from your life is your experience. This experience in turn often reinforces your story. It is important to note that everyone has a different story and that ultimately no one 'lives in the same world'.*

*In certain strands of psychology, these stories are often referred to as 'schema' or 'schemata'. Your schema provides a window into your personality. You can tell a lot about a person's schema by the beliefs they hold and their willingness (or lack thereof) to observe, challenge and reconstruct their schema.*

If 95 per cent of all behaviours, including beliefs, are held in the sub-conscious mind, how does the person's story remains alive, I asked Tao:

*While there are likely to be many inherent falsehoods in your schema; most people hold onto them like clinging to a mast of a sinking ship. And even when they know things aren't working and they are not getting the results they want, many people will hold on for grim death! It seems to be very difficult to surrender, update and replace it [schema] with beliefs that support instead of hinder, by creating a new story that leads you in the direction you do want to go.*

*Further than this, like a mantra, you have told your story over and over again to yourself and others. It is like treading a path through the forest repeatedly and this path becomes your map. It tells you where to go – even if it is in the wrong direction. Just as in the same way you create neural pathways in your brain through repetition. These neural pathways are well and truly established and with your beliefs, your story becomes your reality! Many people really delude themselves into thinking that their beliefs are the truth, that they are factual. What is important to understand is that your experience is an interpretation through your filters with which you experience the world. It often says more about the filters than the actual experience.*

I commented to Tao, at the beginning of the chapter I have inserted a quote that says ,"the map is not the territory".

**Exactly**, *said Tao. Every single human being on this planet experiences the world in his or her own unique way. So you could say no one lives in the same world, Tao laughs, it's a wonder that, while everyone has a different map, we still seem to be able to travel together somehow.*

*It is important to realise that interpretations are processed by a different part of the brain, the feeling part, the limbic system, where feelings and emotional memories lie. The limbic (feeling) part of the brain, the part that is in charge of interpretations, conclusions and assumptions is much faster than the thinking, reasoning part of the brain, the frontal cortex. The feeling part of the brain is very fuel-efficient and can easily over-ride the logical brain.*

*Have you ever tried to convince someone of something that was totally reasonable and logical to you but they just could not see reason because they felt so strongly about their own position? You would look in amazement and scratch your head and say, that is so blatantly obvious, why can't they just see or understand that, it is so simple? Do you know why this is? Because even though the beliefs they hold might be most unhelpful, there is a strong emotional attachment to the story, it feels right.*

*Remember, also that the 'feeling of knowing' over-rides any evidence to the contrary. Feelings are more powerful than logic. If you believe something to be true then it might be hard for anyone to convince you otherwise, unless you are open and willing to having your beliefs challenged.*

So how do we take charge over these unconscious patterns to breakthrough to what it is that we desire, I asked Tao?

*It is only in the space of acknowledgment that transformation can take place. First you need to be aware of and understand that it is just a story that you have constructed without careful deliberation and contemplation. Sadly, the vast majority of people will never become aware of their story, let alone consciously reflect and challenge their story. They will instead live their life according to the same old script, getting the same old results.*

*Becoming aware of the beliefs that stand in the way of what you want, is most important. You can often get clues by the results of your behaviours and actions. The feedback may give you insights in your story.* As your beliefs mainly reside and are kept alive and strong in the limbic part of the brain, you need to address it there.

How do you do this? This part of the brain responds to emotion, visualisation, sound and new evidence.

*Visualise the new behaviour and feel excited about the results you will achieve through employing (yes this is literal, making it work for you) a new belief that matches the results you want to obtain.*

Visualise as if this has already happened, a fait accompli. You need to keep rehearsing and telling yourself the new belief like an actor learning a new script.

*Keep stating the new belief as often as you can just like a mantra.*

*The limbic brain needs repetition to accept the new proposition.*

*Then start looking everywhere you can for the evidence of what is changing as a result of your new story everywhere you can. Put your spotlight on successes, no matter how small and feel great about that emotion.*

I have read that Olympic athletes visualise their performance mentally and the same muscles fire as if they were actually competing in the race or on the field, I said.

***Exactly**, said Tao, one other thing, it is important that your new script, your new story matches what it is you want to achieve. You need to be fully committed that what you want is possible and will become a reality, in other words you have to believe it, even though a part of you might protest and draw you back into the old script. Remember, the greatest resistance will often occur just before the moment of breakthrough!*

Neuroscience research informs us that our brain is changed by every new experience we have and over time our experiences and the subsequent biochemistry (hormonal responses and peptides) created alters our neural pathways guiding us to the experience of fulfilling or not our desires. This pattern then becomes cyclical leading to the same outcomes, time after time. This continual cycle becomes a loop that we can become stuck in: imagine a mouse running around in a maze and you have the general picture.

The pattern interruption can occur when you decide to challenge and change a belief deliberately. Having positive emotional experiences changes the cycle or pattern, over time. That positive emotion can be just appreciating your life right now as it is, no matter what the circumstances are.

Do your beliefs originate beyond your experiences? We know that your beliefs emerge from childhood education, parental or peer guidance and personal experiences. At a deeper level, there is a body of scientific research called epigenetics. Scientists have discovered that we are not genetically programmed, for example, to contract a certain hereditary condition, contrary to previous thinking. Epigenetics is revolutionising scientific assumptions to date, proving that DNA at a cellular level is affected by the environment in which the cell exists and that it can be changed by lifestyle habits. Using this discovery,

Dr Bruce Lipton, a cell biologist has sought to further understand whether epigenetics has a role to play in our beliefs.

Dr Lipton's' research shows that our beliefs live within our cells in DNA structures which have formed an energetic imprint, which is passed on or inherited through family genealogy. This idea is revolutionary when you consider that we all have 'family' beliefs or patterns inherent in our thinking. Attempting to alter one belief can and will affect and shift all the generational thinking in your family from that moment on.

Just imagine the impact of having a familial belief that may run like this: You have to work hard, harder than the next person to succeed or you will surely fail". Perhaps this has been your grandfather's and your father's experience so this continues on through each generation until it reaches you.

We have all experienced family beliefs and their effects. Now just say, you decide …"my life is easy … I do not need to work harder and harder just to succeed."

Epigenetics would now come into play, without your conscious mind conjuring it up.

Our emotions are powerful enough to affect or even change our DNA according to the HeartMath Institute research. This groundbreaking research verified similar studies by Dr Gregg Braden who discovered that DNA can be affected by emotions.

Dr Herbert Benson of Harvard Medical School discovered the 'relaxation response' after determining a methodology to elicit it. He knew that the mental training done by a group of long term meditators could alter their genetic expression. We are far more powerful than we realise. So the key to altering and updating your beliefs lies in your thoughts and your emotions and updating your beliefs to experience what you wish to attract.

I must qualify this statement to say, that not everyone will succeed as an entrepreneur, by applying the formula in this book. There are a number of reasons why. One of the primary reasons lies in the characteristics of an entrepreneur. Entrepreneurs are passionate, focused and driven to achieve their goals. In their personal behaviour, these attributes may manifest as ego-obsessed, arrogant and selfish. A level of self-awareness and emotional intelligence is required to become a successful, well-rounded entrepreneur.

The powerful combination of emotional coherence with a solid belief system in place then forms the basis for an individual to have entrepreneurial breakthroughs.

## KEY POINTS

- Your belief system is powerful and can either hinder or support your progress.
- Beliefs are hidden to the conscious mind and reside in the cellular structures in your DNA.
- Beliefs can be altered dramatically by your thinking and increasing self awareness of your emotional state.
- Visualising and affirming what it is that you desire from a state of positiveness and emotional coherence is the basis for success.
- Using mental rehearsal and becoming mindful of all your conscious thoughts, forms the basis for creating entrepreneurial success.

# CHAPTER 4
## The Energy of Passion

 *There is no passion to be found playing small – in settling for a life that is less than the one you are capable of living.*

NELSON MANDELA

My research on entrepreneurs showed that their one of the key points of differentiation was to be passionate about what it is that they want to achieve. In fact, the entrepreneurs' passionate attention not only creates the future business opportunity, it is brought into reality by sustaining their level of passion, with intentionality.

I interviewed Daniel Carlin, the founder of Elevate™ a health and wellness clinic and corporate health provider after meeting him some time ago. At the time I met Dan, Elevate™ was the first 'one stop' shop providing medical and complementary modalities through their clinic in Sydney CBD, whilst providing organisations with health checks and education in preventative health for their employees. Elevate™ was growing rapidly and to meet market demand it commenced a capital raising to fund an expansion programme to launch new clinics around Australia and the Asia Pacific region.

I was interested to know the progress of the business and how this young entrepreneur was dealing with the demands of a corporate entity's regime, which had been quite foreign to him when he started the business. Daniel's early career was in film sound recording and his personal interest in fitness ensured that he was a regular at the gym. He decided to make a career change and studied personal training. His clients were largely stressed executives who were working long hours and had little to no understanding of health, nutrition or the basics of living a balanced life. He found himself being asked for advice about how to have more energy, increased resilience and lowered stress at work and at home.

He visited clinics in Sydney's' CBD looking for answers to his clients' questions and discovered that they focused on medical services, repairing poor health rather than preventive health. Daniel had seen an opportunity. Following his intuition, he researched his potential competition, and started building the new clinic, to be named Elevate™.

As he told me, at the time financing and signing a long-term lease in a city high-rise and funding renovations to turn the premises into a clinic was a challenge. He enlisted the help of, as he called them, – the three Fs – family, friends and fools!

This unique one stop shop with large organisations employing Elevate™ to be their health provider together with integrative practitioners improving the health outcomes of the employees was an instant success.

At the time of our interview, the Sydney clinic was eight years old, I asked Daniel, where the business was up to now and whether his personal resolve to develop the clinics successfully was still strong. In the intervening years, Daniel had recognised that he needed to involve other people who had experience in growing global businesses. A board was appointed with a new managing director, chair and directors to take the business to the next level of expansion. The first step was to make sure that the business was ready for this growth, spending time on systems, governance and process as a new priority. At this time, the competition for the corporate health dollar had increased dramatically with major health providers moving into the space. New thinking was required about alternative business models that were different to Daniels' original plan.

> *Elevate™ is really the first serious business, there's a Board, there's financials, there's a lot more rigour and systems, and also investment and cost and we've got shareholders and there's a lot more involved, all that stuff. I've definitely found in the more recent years I don't act as quickly and intuitively as I used to when I was younger. I'm finding there's a lot more thinking and analytical stuff going on for me now, and that actually can be quite paralysing.*

I asked Daniel, as a follower of his intuition in developing this business, had he experienced a single Aha moment?

> *There's been an element of what feels right for us and what we feel is true for us, and then also listening to the marketplace. And I think that's how my whole life's been in terms of opportunities that have come up. It's been because there's been a need or something that's pulled me in that direction rather than the heavens opened and, oh, that's the moment.*

Your original breakthrough may take a lot longer to become a viable market proposition than you first imagined or the market need may be different by the time you are ready to take off with your vision. An entrepreneur will pursue the end result against almost any and all odds. This passion can be both a blessing and a curse for a true entrepreneur. From my research, this was no surprise as serial entrepreneurs like Daniel, driven by a passionate vision, often feel frustrated with the finer details of implementation of the plan and the speed at which it unfolds.

More importantly, you must have the ability to nurture yourself at the same time, when you are most likely working extraordinary hours, never taking holidays, thinking about the business you are creating continually, possibly losing friends and family as a result of your single-minded narrow focus. These are some possible downsides of becoming an entrepreneur. As Daniel grew the initial business of Elevate™, ironically, he suffered a health crisis. His drive to pursue his vision meant that he was running too fast.

In his words:

*I basically burnt myself out after setting Elevate™ up, and it really took me down. I ended up needing medication. I needed a lot of health support, emotionally and physically. I was just destroyed, and it's taken me this last two years to rebuild it [my health]. A part of that rebuild was because I was always at a million miles an hour; I had to learn how to slow down a bit. Up until the age of 32, I had just gone flat out, and if you think about what I like socially, it's all the extreme sports; it's all the things that go fast, racing motorcycles, snowboarding, and surfing. And if I was running fast, it wasn't relaxing. I didn't do anything that was slow.*

*So after I had that health scare, it kind of really forced me to go, okay, I need to somehow slow down a bit. I actually got diagnosed as an adrenalin junkie.*

*I used to drink two or three really industrial strength coffees every day, and I didn't need them, I was already running at a million miles an hour.*

Research informs that your body becomes addicted to the chemicals and hormones we produce; for Daniel, adrenaline and cortisol were the most potent combination.

Inevitably a loop happens when the cortisol keeps being circulated in the body, stopping you from being able to relax and rest when you need it the most.

Daniel learnt new ways of managing his burnout and adrenal fatigue, adopting meditation and relaxation practices, yoga and hypnotherapy learning how to slow down. This time allowed him to develop new opportunities.

*Over these last two years, it gave me a real understanding of what it must be like for so many people working in these corporate towers out here. There are stats [statistics] now on adrenal fatigue and even sleep, you know, sleep apnoea is one of the biggest undiagnosed diseases out there, and sleep affects our health so much, and then obviously off the back of our health is our performance and productivity.*

The change of the original business plan and his own health challenge saw Daniel make a decision to look beyond his original creation to build other businesses in the wellness industry.

*I've always been someone who likes to create and build things. I'm now at the point where I'm trying to make the decision of which direction to take, and I have a new business idea, and that's probably a lot of that's coming from my intuition of what I feel is right for me.*

> When I think about it, most of the time in new businesses, especially when you're trail blazing or you're doing something that hasn't been done before, you don't have the data there, you don't have the market research there, you can try and do some market research but typically it's fabricated – it's something you've gone out and created rather than seeing what the market says about it. Entrepreneurs, if they didn't have an intuitive sense, would never take action. If they didn't go with that intuition and take that leap they'd never build a business because if you were completely logical, you'd never get started. If you were waiting until it was a hundred percent right, you'd never go. My attitude has always been 70 or 80 per cent's good enough – launch and figure out the rest along the way.

One aspect of creating the success you desire, is the ability to not just be passionate, it is to focus your attention solely on what it is you desire. The ability to focus according to Daniel Goleman, the Harvard professor, who researched and later coined the term emotional intelligence, says is lacking for many people today as our attention is frayed by multiple demands and distractions from our many electronic devices.

One serial entrepreneur, I interviewed, Simon Bailey who has an early background in commercial law and investment banking has a unique perspective on distraction. Simon is known for the incisive thinking that he brings to any venture, whether it is a start-up, turnaround and restructure activities, strategy and change and implementation. Simon related his well-honed techniques to singularly focus on whatever he is working on:

> It would have been in the late 80s, I had a brain full of stuff. I realized that my brain was at a capacity, so I bought a computer and taught myself how to use it and I dumped everything in my brain into the

*computer. Suddenly I had an empty brain box! I worked out very quickly that most of the things people put into their brain is clutter. If you take me to a trivia night, I will be the most useless person on the team. I have no trivia. If you take me to anything which says, how do you fix a problem whether it's electrical or computers or the human body, or nature – anything you know that works, I can probably fix it for you. I remember the patterns about how to organise stuff and when you remember you know the sort of root-level cause of this stuff, it's all quite simple. You then extrapolate from as many facts as you can consume. I have a brain full of thinking patterns and I have a brain full of understanding cause and effect relationships. I have absolutely nothing else in there, so when I go to take a new business on which has been my life's work or a new project, I can dump 5,000 or 10,000 pages worth of data in, think my way through and usually don't sleep for about 96 or 140 hours. I'm quite comfortable doing that because I don't sleep much and I don't get angry when I'm not sleeping, I just relax through it and let my brain do what it does. You discard some of that which is irrelevant and start to take on more stuff. At the end of a project I dump all of it. Now so that's the thinking piece and the prepared brain piece. I start the day with a raft of exercises and Tai Chi which is very much about clearing everything out.*

Simon practices what we intuitively know: attention is a limited capacity – four bits of information is the upper limit that we are able to hold in our conscious mind – this has shrunk from the seven bits previously agreed by cognitive scientists.[i]  His practice of focused attention and regular Tai Chi, has re-trained his brain. One of the most effective ways to improve your attention to focus is to meditate regularly.

---

i   Moskowitz, Clara. *"Mind's Limited Found : 4 Things at Once"*. Live Science. April 27, 2008. *www.livescience.com/2493-mind-limit-4.html*

The latest research shows that meditation can help you to improve your ability to concentrate in two ways. First, it can make you better at focusing on something specific while ignoring distractions. Second, it can make you more capable of noticing what is happening around you, giving you a fuller perspective on the present moment.

Some of the most fascinating research on how meditation affects attention is being conducted by Antoine Lutz, PhD, an associate scientist at the Waisman Laboratory for Brain Imaging and Behaviour at the University of Wisconsin at Madison, in collaboration with Richard Davidson and the Laboratory for Affective Neuroscience at the University of Wisconsin. Their work has shown that concentration meditation, in which the meditator focuses complete attention on one thing, such as counting the breaths or gazing at an object, activates regions of the brain that are critical for controlling attention. This is true even amongst novice meditators who receive only brief training. Experienced meditators show even stronger activation in these regions. This you would expect, if meditation trains the brain to pay attention. However extremely experienced meditators (who have more than 44,000 hours of meditation practice) show less activation in these regions, even though their performance on attention tasks is better. The explanation for this, in Lutz's view, is that the meditation training can eventually help reduce the effort it takes to focus your attention. "This would be consistent with traditional accounts of progress in meditation practice. Sustaining focus becomes effortless," Lutz says. This suggests that people can immediately enhance concentration by learning a simple meditation technique, and that practice creates even more progress.[ii]

Here is a simple meditation technique allowing you to focus your breathing through the different parts of your body, literally

---

[ii] *www.mindful.org/the-science/neuroscience/your-brain-on-meditation*

commanding your body to relax with a focused attention on the brief. You may use this technique at any time of the day to relax, fully and completely. Do not use this technique whilst driving or in any situation where you need to be fully alert. You may choose to record this technique for use on your smart phone or tablet device, if you wish. Make sure you will not be disturbed at this time, turn off your phone and make sure that you are seated in a quiet place.

## Practising Deep Relaxation

*Begin by closing your eyes ... allow your mind to become clear of all thoughts, and focus on your breathing ... Breathing easily and deeply ... Easily and deeply ... Breathing relaxation into your body, and breathing away any tension*

*Breathing relaxation into your mind and breathing away any thoughts*

*Very gently, begin to withdraw yourself from the outside environment*

*Withdraw yourself from your surroundings*

*Withdraw yourself from any remaining thoughts*

*Withdraw yourself into yourself*

*Into your own silence*

*Into your own peace and relax*

*Allow the muscles of your face, to relax*

*Your forehead ... the muscles around your eyes ... the muscles behind your eyes, your lips ... tongue ... throat and ... jaw ... all ... deeply relaxed*

*Allow the relaxation to flow down through your neck, into your shoulders, you may wish to move your shoulders, to relax ...*

*Allow the relaxation to flow down both your arms, all the way to your fingertips*

*Allow the relaxation to flow into your chest, and down your back and spine*

*Allowing the muscles of your back to just ... let go*

*You let go ... just let go ... you ... just ... let ... go*

*Take the relaxation to your torso and allow it to go deep into your stomach*

*Right into the very centre of your body*

*Right into the very centre of your being*

*Allow the relaxation to flow down your hips and pelvis*

*Down your legs to your ankles and right into your feet and toes*

*So now you are deeply relaxed you are experiencing your whole body as deeply relaxed ... quiet and still*

*Experience the feeling of being deeply relaxed ...*

*Pause for a few minutes or longer*

*As you feel this deep relaxation, find a symbol, word, phrase that describes how you are feeling right now.*

SOURCE: ANNA WISE, THE HIGH PERFORMANCE MIND

## KEY POINTS

- The entrepreneurs' passion creates the future business opportunity, and it becomes reality by sustaining their level of passion, with intention.
- An entrepreneur will pursue the end result against almost any and all odds.
- Remember to maintain a balance between your passion for your business and enjoying your life.
- The ability to renew your energy and nurture yourself is critical to your long- term success – adrenal stress and burnout will not serve you or your business.
- Focused attention is enhanced and your brain changed by a regular meditation or relaxation practice – find a technique that works for you!

# CHAPTER 5
## The Role of the Heart

 *What lies behind us and what lies before us are small matters compared to what lies within us. And when we bring what is within us out into the world, miracles happen.*

RALPH WALDO EMERSON

You will by now begin to understand the formula for creating consciously your new entrepreneurial business or in fact whatever it is that you desire. We have reviewed what keeps you from achieving success, for example, your beliefs and early programming – now it is time for you to know how to consciously create what you desire, every time.

When Professor Murray Gillin was researching entrepreneurs and their ability to create successful business, he was initially surprised by some of his findings, which included the role of the heart.

As Murray told me:

*I came across the work of the HeartMath Institute® in the US. The HeartMath Institute® have been studying the human heart [for the past thirty years] and had developed simple tools to enable people to lower their stress levels and improve their levels of creativity and intuitive insight. I contacted them as they had done significant research into how intuitive information is perceived by the heart prior to the insight reaching the brain. To achieve this, they had developed a means of analysing the electro-physiological issue.*

*The HeartMath Institute® had discovered the most effective way to measure different emotional states was to study heart rate variability [the change in the rate between individual heart beats].*

*HeartMath Institute® have found that heart rate variability patterns are extremely responsive to emotions, and heart rhythms tend to become more ordered or coherent during positive emotional states and incoherent or disordered during negative emotional states. The term psycho-physiological coherence is used to refer to states in which a high degree of order and harmony in the emotional domain translates as increased coherence in physiological patterns and processes.*[i]

---

[i] Bradley, Raymond Trevor. "The Psychophysiology of Entrepreneurial Intuition: A Quantum-Holographic Theory". Institute for Whole Social Science, HeartMath Institute®, California, USA and e-Motion Institute, Auckland, New Zealand.

# THE ROLE OF THE HEART

**The HeartMath Institute® determined that the heart has its own intelligence network which can learn, remember and produce feelings – enabling it to act independently of the brain.** These attributes, until recently, were nearly universally understood to be solely in the brain's dominion.[ii]

The conversation on the role of the heart immediately brought to my mind romantic novels often portraying women where the hearts' role had been the culprit leading them into less than desirable situations.

Does the heart have a unique intelligence separate to the brain? The traditional view has been that the brain directed the heart's responses. Or is it simply a Newtonian linear view that the brain is a superior part of the body?

The HeartMath Institute® and my research concluded that our intuition is a unique form of sensory perception that is connected to and constantly communicating with the universal field of energy. Some scientists believe that the brain is simply a sophisticated retrieval mechanism, accessing all information that is held in the quantum field. You may like to think of it as a giant database.

Research conducted at the HeartMath Institute® concluded that the heart is the most powerful generator of electromagnetic energy in the human body, producing the largest rhythmic electromagnetic field of any of the body's organs. The heart's electrical field is about 60 times greater in amplitude than the electrical activity generated by the brain.

---

ii  Scharmer, Otto. *"Theory of U: Leading from the Emerging Future"*. MIT Sloan School of Management.

Furthermore, the magnetic field produced by the heart is of greater strength than the field generated by the brain, and can be detected a number of feet away from the body, in all directions.[iii]

## Electromagnetic Field of the Heart

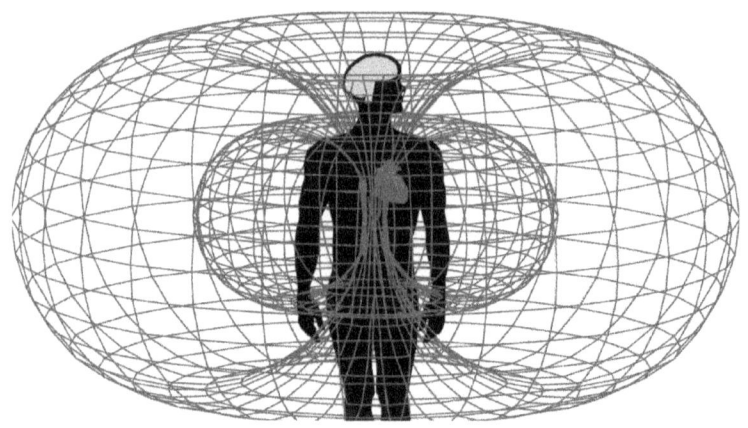

This means that we directly affect our environment and we affect each person that we come into contact with as we interact with their electromagnetic field!

Have you ever had the experience of feeling positive and happy until you met someone who was unhappy and pessimistic and you walked away feeling less positive? That is the result of the direct effect we have on each other through interaction with their electro-magnetic fields.

In a business meeting, you may have people who are expressing a negative viewpoint and are unwilling to adopt a more positive

---

iii HeartMath Institute®. *"The Science of the Heart"*. *www.heartmath.org*

view; everyone in the room feels the mood shift. This process of the electromagnetic fields of the heart penetrating each other is called 'entrainment'.

The heart's magnetic field literally entrains with every other person's magnetic field that you are in contact with within a few feet distance. More importantly this entrainment enables an entrepreneur to access the quantum field of opportunity (refer Chapter 2) Murray's research determined that:

> *When the entrepreneur calms his mind and feelings, and adopts a heart-focused state of positive emotion directed to the object, a global shift to psycho-physiological coherence is induced which optimises attention resonance with the incoming quantum level information from the object of interest.*
>
> *Such attunement brings the outgoing wave field of attentional energy from the entrepreneurs' psycho-physiological systems into harmonic resonance with the incoming wave field of energy from the object. The harmonic resonance between the two wave fields of energy creates an optimal channel for communication of nonlocal information.*
>
> *The more the entrepreneur can maintain coherent attentional interest directed to the object of interest, the more his body's psycho-physiological systems will have access to this implicit field of quantum holographic information and hence the greater the intuitive foreknowledge about the object of interest.*
>
> *Remember, we are not consciously aware of this perfectly functioning system that is in place organising our heart beating and our breathing patterns. This autonomic system is made up of cells, molecules, atoms, and sub-atomic particles, which are essentially energy.*

***Everything is energy and vibrates at a sub-atomic level outside our normal conscious awareness.*** *Energy is made up of atoms and molecules broken down into waves (energy) and particles (physical matter) that have the same qualities. Nothing is solid, and static, matter is purely energy or frequency patterns of information, allowing human beings to affect their environment at a sub-atomic level. And when I speak to entrepreneurs [about my research] they are excited. They almost always say, this makes sense to us, How can we find out more?*

*Whenever I speak with hard headed cognitive academics, they say 'can't happen'. Now that intrigues me. Academics and researchers should want to explore new ideas, not shut them off. The academic process knocks creativity out of you. We have become so imbued with what I call linear thinking. And we have forgotten that life is not linear. It's a complex holistic system.*

The hearts' intelligence through its electro-magnetic field is communicating with the universal energy field, scanning its so called database for potential opportunities.

Murray continued, quoting directly from his research paper:

*The entrepreneurs' passionate attention – that is the biological energy activated in his emotional connection to the object of interest (e.g. the quest for future opportunities in a certain field of business) attunes him/her to the object's unfolding pattern of activity and to the implicit order of its future potential. Both the pattern of activity and the potential future order are spectrally encoded as a quantum hologram in a field of potential energy as implicit information in a domain apart from space and time. At a biological level, the body's psycho-physiological systems generate numerous fields of energy at various frequencies that interpenetrate the field of potential energy.*

# THE ROLE OF THE HEART

From Dr Ray Bradley's research, his conclusion verifies the formula previously studied:

*The act of conscious perception requires both an incoming wave field of sensory information about the object and an outgoing wave field of attentional energy. Based on recent research, it is clear that more than the brain is involved in the act of attention. The body's psycho-physiological systems generate numerous fields of energy, at various frequencies, that radiate outwards from the body as wave fields in all directions. Of these, the heart generates the most powerful rhythmic electromagnetic field. Not only does a massive deceleration in the heart's pattern of rhythmic activity occur at the moment of mental attention, which would generate a powerful change recorded in the outgoing wave field, but it is also clear from recent research that nonlocal perception is related to the percipient's degree of emotional arousal generated by an object. It is the individual's passion or "rapt attention"–biological energy activated in his emotional connection to the object of his interest–that generates the outgoing attentional wave directed to the object.[iv]*

Wow! I said, if I translate this into plain English, when I use not only my thought, my emotion and my passion in a state of calmness, envisioning with clarity, then this will allow the potential opportunity to occur?

Why is this information not head-line news? This is ground breaking, I said excitedly.

---

[iv] *"Beta, Alpha, Theta, Delta are descriptions of the amount of electrical activity in the brain at any time measured as signals in Hz. Alpha and Theta are more relaxed states of activity compared to Beta brainwave state". http://eocinstitute.org/meditation/brainwave_charts_brainwave_patterns/*

The opportunity to meet a real life practitioner of the ability to deliberately access information from the quantum field confirmed what I had learnt from Murray occurred in my next interview.

I had interviewed Michael Rennie, the Managing Partner, of the global management consultancy, McKinsey & Company for my first book on intuition. When I first met Michael, he was based in New York in 2004. Michael had developed a highly successful culture change programme for multi-national organisations in Australia and was extending this work to McKinsey US and European clients.

Michael is an extraordinary individual. His personal study and interests included philosophy, languages and economics. He was awarded a Rhodes scholarship, becoming a lawyer prior to joining McKinsey & Co. In his early thirties, he was diagnosed with cancer, and was told by his doctors his life may not exceed 12 months. After a period of deep introspection, while undergoing chemotherapy, Michael adopted additional health regimes including meditation, visualisation and positive psychology practices to heal his body of cancer.

Fully recovered and back at McKinsey, Michael was fascinated by his own journey of change and recovery, and sought to incorporate his learnings for individuals within organisations to work with more authenticity and passion. Michael established a new part of the McKinsey service portfolio for its clients working with individuals and teams in organisations to develop a high-performance culture, focusing on individual mindset.

Michael challenged business leaders' modes of behavior with traditionally aggressive and overly competitive behaviours, asking people to examine their own beliefs, values and meaning in their professional and personal lives. One of the keys to the success of the program was that it enabled people to tap into how they were feeling, not just about their work, about their personal lives.

We had discussed the subject of intuition in great detail in my first interview. When I met Michael again in 2010, I already knew the answer to my first question as Michael is a person who is very aware of intuition and uses it actively in his daily life. He expanded on this subject relating how intuition fits into the overall mode of thinking in his view:

> *I have come to realise that there are a number of different modes of thinking. There is a logical mode of thinking where you can sit down and work through all the pieces, which is a lot of what we do here [at McKinsey]. Then there is inductive and deductive thinking within that. We get trained a lot in those different thinking modes and how to communicate that to clients – that is a big part of the model here.*
>
> *There is also feeling, and the more you come to realise that thinking is not just analytical/rational – [it] rather has an irrational and feeling component to it. So I have learnt to be quite sensitive to what I am feeling, when I am thinking, because the feeling comes first, often, and actually creates the thoughts. All the research seems to support that.*
>
> *You start to realise that there is analytical logic and feeling. And there is an aspect of feeling, which can often be very logical and it actually directs you.*
>
> *So when you go, "why am I feeling this?", it actually directs you towards certain logic, or it can appear illogical and you can't work out in the moment why you are feeling that. There is something going on that you need to be aware of, or take account of, and there is a deeper form of thinking. I call it intuition or knowingness. The way I*

*think about it is very much a physics analogy. We have a Newtonian world of physics, which is large objects that move very slowly – zero to 200 cycles per second, and then you have the world of the quantum, which is very small objects moving at 500,000 cycles per second, and everything is operating in a quantum reality.*

*You then go into the deeper side, that there is actually information. And everything that is happening is actually recorded as information in the quantum through wave action and theory. There is a way in which you can tap into the quantum. The logical is very much at the Newtonian level, and there is a quantum level of thinking, which is intuition. For me it is about tapping into the field of quantum energy – so how does that work?*

*It's like a 'U'. I did a lot of work with people like Otto Scharmer [v], who has developed the Theory of U, when I was working in the States. It is a nice way of thinking about it. Essentially, the key to intuitive thinking, to me, is the physiology – three bodies – the physical, mental and emotional.*

*You have a physical body, the lungs, mental–emotional brain and nervous system. The feeling part of it – thinking – is happening in the emotional body, and then it is coming into the physical body as action, or the stimulus is coming from the emotional body. And there is a third body, which is an energetic body.*

*The key is how you tap into the third body, and the way you tap into that is essentially for me a two-prong process -- the first is that you have got to intimately connect yourself with the subject matter, essentially you have got to be in it, intimately.*

---

[v] Scharmer, Otto, *Theory of U: Leading from the Emerging Future*. MIT Sloan School of Management.

*Once you are deeply in it, it's like the veils between the worlds – you have got to go into it, **and there is a point at which you sort of let go into it**, and you wait for what comes – it is like a small voice that comes to you.*

I asked Michael how do you engender that – is it through meditation or relaxation techniques? And could you give me an example of where you have experienced a major insight or breakthrough that has affected your life – professionally or personally?

*The first thing I always do is get into a quiet space – you have to get out of the active Beta mind into the quieter mind. Then when you are in the quiet space, you have the topic that you want to work with, that you are passionately involved with, and you essentially go into that. It does not work unless you are quiet first, so meditative practice or some form of quietening is important.*

*Once in that place, then I just essentially close my eyes and sit with it and I will actually start. It is like a freewheeling thinking about it without any need or concentration. So you take all the fear out of the process, and it is just like you are playing with or sitting with the topic.*

*This is how I learnt how to do it. And then just let go, and let it go wherever it goes. Then you wait for it to come, and whatever comes is quiet, relative to the noise of the mind. So you have to be very thoughtful and just go with whatever comes. And as it starts to come, you just go with whatever comes.*

*For instance, if I need to write a document, I will not write in Beta. [I] sit quietly, go to Alpha/Theta imagine the whole thing and just sit with it. It will start to reorganise itself and all the pieces will come together in a beautiful way and I can see the whole thing or a speech.*

*The way I write every speech is that I sit and imagine the audience – who are these people, why [have] they come here? They are unique; this has never happened before. I have been asked to come and be with them. What is it that they are calling for? And that, essentially, is what I am sitting with. What comes is sometimes unexpected, and what happens is the whole thing about why I am there will become clear to me and the speech will unfold out of that.*

*I do this every day. When I wake up in the morning, I spend the first 15 or 20 minutes sitting quietly, imagining the day, all the things that have to happen, thinking about the difficult things. Quite often in our work – we are working on something at the moment, it is very big, famous Australian company going through a lot of change where we can actually help them with that, where there are a lot of moving parts, board members, different things, very complex – we know what we need to do.*

*When there are too many moving parts, I know that I cannot work it out in my logical mind because these are complex, adaptive systems that are beyond logic, per se, immediate logic, so you have to use this approach. I will essentially sit there and start imagining all the pieces of the puzzle and I will just think it through. I will just sit with it, just start to form – I think of it as going down a 'Y' formation, and suddenly all the pieces happen and it feels like it is becoming orchestrated. It becomes bigger than it ever could and there is a lot of trust that is required to do that; it works every time.*

As an advanced practitioner of knowing how to access his intuition and logical thinking with his feelings, Michael cautioned that, in his experience, the criteria for success is always to intend to be of service, to serve the greater good. As he said:

# THE ROLE OF THE HEART

*The big thing for me is, at the core, there is a feeling of being Francis of Assisi – his famous comment – let me be of service. It is really a question of what is required, because if I am a consultant walking into a company, I am there to help – to help make something happen.*

*My personal journey has been about learning how to operate in all three and learning how to move from one to the other – seeking to do well. It is a journey – logical thinking is vital.*

*You have got to trust your gut feeling as an entrepreneur because if you don't, it will come and bite you. Generally, as an entrepreneur, you cannot make massive mistakes early; whereas, if you are in a big company, just the weight of the business will keep everything going. In an entrepreneurial situation, you do not have that, so you really have to rely on [your gut feeling] early. Afterwards, I knew that, and then intuition is key because of the uncertainty – you cannot "logic" your way through uncertainty.*

*It's quantum, so you have to go into the quantum. And I have the same view of entrepreneurial things as a consultant, which is, if what you are doing is of service, if your entrepreneurial venture is helping in some way – it is about finding out what is being called for and you are crafting something, and you can feel it crafting something. So being of service – what makes that important to intuition is that it actually is what opens up the 'Field'.*

*For me, a lot of what this is about, from a physics point of view, is that you have the mental-emotional body, you have the quantum body, and the quantum body physiologically is in the same space as the emotional body. So it is communicating with where the energy is coming in and going out. What prevents that from happening – if you have an egoist self sense, you are actually cutting your energy field off from others.*

Importantly, Professor Murray Gillin reports from his research in Cambridge that all the serial entrepreneurs interviewed expressed an extremely high level of 'commitment to serve' and 'give-back' to society. This strong 'harmonic' frequency is a defining characteristic of the successful and intuitive entrepreneur.

## KEY POINTS

- Intuition is a unique form of sensory perception that is connected to and constantly communicating with the universal field of energy
- The magnetic field produced by the heart is of greater strength than the field generated by the brain, and can be detected a number of feet away from the body, in all directions.
- The more the entrepreneur can maintain coherent attention directed to the object of interest, the more his body's psycho physiological systems will have access to this implicit field of quantum holographic information
- The heart's intelligence through its electro-magnetic field is communicating with the universal energy field, scanning it's so called database for potential opportunities.
- When you use thought, emotion and passion in a state of calmness, envisioning with clarity, the potential opportunity will occur due to the action between the two wave fields of energy creating an optimal channel for communication of nonlocal information.
- Being willing to serve the highest good of all concerned is what opens up the 'Field'.

# CHAPTER 6
## Focused Intention

 *If you form and hold your intent strongly enough, it becomes true.*

SRIKUMAR RAO

I have often wondered how intuition and intention may be linked. After the intuitive insight has occurred, what next? Intention is the final step in the process of developing successful entrepreneurial breakthroughs. In this context, the meaning of intention is far greater than a desire to proceed with an intuitive idea or opportunity.

Intentionality means the deliberate focus on a desire or idea that ultimately can bring it into reality [human intention affecting the physical properties of materials]. There is an emerging science around the power of focused human intention that proves that human beings are fully capable of altering physical reality. Experiments conducted at the Institute of Noetic Sciences (IONS) in California, and at Princeton Engineering Anomalies Research Lab (PEAR) have shown that focused human thought has the ability to change physical mass. Our thoughts really do interact and affect our physical world, creating change at a sub-atomic level.

Emeritus Professor William A. Tiller is a pioneer in the study of human intentionality. Tiller spent 34 years as a Professor in Stanford University's Department of Materials Science plus an additional nine years as an advisory physicist with the Westinghouse Research Laboratories. A Fellow of the American Academy for the Advancement of Science, he has published over 250 scientific papers, three books and several patents. At the same time, Tiller has researched the power of human intention as a measurable thermodynamic variable, such as heat or gravity. In this area, he has published more than 150 scientific papers and four seminal books, two DVDs, 30 free white papers and a quantitative model of ongoing experiments designed to understand what he names as psycho-energetic science. As a consequence of his research interests and findings, he has been likened to a modern day Galileo causing the prevailing scientists to radically re-evaluate their understandings of reality.

As I discovered when I interviewed Tiller, his re-evaluation was not welcomed by some of his scientific peers. Yet Tiller has continued to promote the message that **human beings affect their environment, at a sub-atomic level**. Tiller's message is an extra-ordinary one with the potential to change all scientific assumptions to date. My interview with Bill was conducted on Skype from his home in Arizona, USA. The interview was all-encompassing about the power of human intention and the role of intuition and intentionality. I have reprinted it here with minor editing. It is a powerful testament to a man whose life has been devoted to the work of intentionality and the science behind it.

Bill's opening statement summarises his findings:

*For the last four hundred years, an unstated assumption of science is that human intention cannot affect what we call 'physical reality'. Our experimental research of the past decade shows that, for today's world and under the right conditions, this assumption is no longer correct. We humans are much more than we think we are and Psychoenergetic Science continues to expand the proof of it.* [i]

Forty years ago, Tiller and his wife started practising meditation with the intention to be more focused and to develop more insight into their decision-making. Bill discovered much more than the power of mediation to calm and focus his mind.

I first asked Bill how his interest had developed in exploring intuition and intentionality, from his background as a traditional scientist.

*I was indeed [a traditional scientist] for 34 years at Stanford and, before that nine years in the industry at the Westinghouse research laboratory.*

*My work comes from a level of intuition but it manifests as specific intention.*

*I had a Guggenheim Fellowship to go to England with my family for a sabbatical. I read this little book, Psychic Discoveries behind the Iron Curtain, by Ostrander and Schroeder. I knew a lot about the Russian work but I was impressed with the scope of that work. As I was reading it, I asked the question "How might the universe be constructed to allow this crazy seeming kind of stuff to naturally co-exist with the orthodox science that I was doing with my PhD students at Stanford every day?"*

*I started writing the books of my conventional science but this particular question kept coming to mind and it began to aggravate*

---

i   *www.tillerinstitute.com*

*me. I decided that I must find out an answer to this question. I took that question into my meditative state and I held it like a brick, like a supplicant, asking for an answer. There would be some insight that we would each [my wife & I] have when we came out of meditation. My wife is not at all scientific, but she is very intuitive. I took those insights upstairs to my work room and I would ask myself questions all day: is there any aspect of physics, experimental physics that violates these insights? I didn't care about the theoretical aspects that can be easily wrong, but experimental data is where the truth is as far as I'm concerned. The next day we would go into meditation and we would hold not only the main brick, but all these new things that had come up and then there would be all these other things come out of meditation. We did that every day for six months and at the end of six months I had an answer to the question; I had a model. We had allowed the orthodox science to join with we'll call this psycho-energetic science, the issue was you've got to get outside of distance/time, if you want to answer this category of question.*

*I looked around to see who I could get to work on that, who was really committed to do that; it might take as much as a lifetime and finally I decided that it had to be me. There wasn't really anyone I could palm it off on because it was pretty strange stuff to most people. I was comfortable with it; it felt pretty natural and reasonable to me. So I decided, how can I do this, I have got to keep my job to feed my family and this would take a lot of time. I had to give up being Department Chair and my government and professional committees and then I'd have a block of time. My wife agreed that she would take care of the children whilst I could do as much of this work on the side. It's like starting another branch of science and I divided the time into three equal parts. The first was experiential development of self, that was a key issue, keep experiencing, and keep trying to feel this aspect of nature. The second was to keep asking the questions of how the universe might be constructed to enrich that picture that*

*I had developed. The third was to do experiments to keep the theory honest. That began in 1971 and I've been doing it ever since.*

Bill, did you bring in other colleagues into this? Did you talk to other scientists?

*When I told them I was going to give up being Department Chair in order to do this, they thought I was crazy. The university wasn't particularly happy because I was a financial rainmaker in that department and, it was known that I was taking this path in addition to my orthodox path, I lost all kinds of opportunities, both to gather money and to become a member of the National Academy. That was all too much for them and it was basically too much for the university because universities depend upon money given to them by wealthy people, normally those who have been very successful in the conventional world. They think very conventionally and they would think that I was kind of crazy and the university would therefore lose money because they kept this Professor around doing orthodox work and also doing this other stuff, even if it wasn't in the university, it was all outside the university. They would be upset about it but so long as I did my day job well, published and graduated as many PhD students as anyone else and did my classes then they tolerated it.*

It's extraordinary isn't it because the role of science is to discover?

*It's supposed to be open and I made the mistake of believing that, that was an illusion of mine, I believed that if I continued to do world-class work in my orthodox area, which they just loved, then they would perhaps be open enough to look at this other but they couldn't, they just couldn't bring themselves to do that. It wasn't just the work itself that was so difficult for them to comprehend, but of course they'd lose pecking order, they'd lose status in certain ways.*

Bill, how are they today, are they still the same in your view?

*They're still the same; the orthodox community is still very much like in the days of Galileo where the Theocrats would not even look through the telescope at this experimental data. Our orthodox community think that well, we've got the Higgs Boson, we're really near the end of the trail. All that does is really give closure to the standard model which is based on electro magnetism.*

*The limit of all of our measuring devices is the velocity of light from electromagnetism, yet the physical background, where most of the energy really is in nature is faster than light – from my work.*

*So, in essence, again it just shows where the orthodox community is; they're doing a great job in the area where they are, but that area can't touch consciousness, it can't touch the higher quality of the humans. That means you can't deal with anything that is higher dimensionality than distance/time, which is a four-dimensional frame.*

*We created a device that could hold an intention and then we imprinted the intention from a deep meditative state; we go into, probably the void. It's like again being a supplicant to nature and intending with many details of course to do a specific thing.*

*We showed that using our intention host devices, we could change the properties of materials in specific ways, the first one was to investigate pH- the acid alkaline balance of water, so we would take pure water as a standard and the intention was to increase the pH by 1 pH unit, well that's a factor of 10 in hydrogen ion concentration, it's also 23.6 million electron volts change, so we were able to do that with no chemical additions. Then we took the same water and we reduced it by 1 pH unit again with no chemical additions. They were the two simple experiments easier to do. The next was to take a liver enzyme, alkaline phosphatase and to increase its chemical activity significantly.*

*What we did, is we conditioned the space to the next higher level of reality and we just exposed the liver enzyme for 30 minutes to that space and then took it out and measured it again and found that we could increase the chemical activity by 30 per cent. These were remarkably robust experiments and showed unequivocally that in today's world the Descartes assumption which is still held unconsciously by the scientific community is totally wrong. It's still held because it's at the unconscious level now.*

*Of course the discoveries are revolutionary, they turn every type of thinking about, whether they're about invention, health, and all aspects of life could be radically altered.*

*Descartes made this assumption about 1600. Roughly the assumption was, no human qualities of consciousness, intention, emotion, mind or spirit can significantly influence a well-designed target experiment in physical reality.*

*Now that was a really good assumption for that day because it was important to separate the issue between – is it science or is it religion – and that took more than 100 years for the Theocrats to accept science, a scientific path.*

*With any significant new paradigm shift, it takes a long time. This one will probably be even longer, because they've made such great strides in distance and time-related phenomenon that are all stored in the velocity of light. Then there are various conclusions and assumptions, even made by the best of them, like Einstein, that nothing can go faster than light. We can show that that isn't true; therefore, we have to lay it out very carefully, the pieces of data that show that these assumptions are not true in today's world.*

*It may take a long time, but we can enhance every business in the world that exists today by some degree, and create new opportunities and new business.*

*We have learnt how to broadcast intention over long distances, that is up to 6,000 miles so far. We have been able to broadcast an intention to an experimental group of 520 people spread over maybe 10,000 square miles, to significantly reduce depression and anxiety in them with an eight-month broadcast to them and again, the broadcast appears to be an entirely different energy than electromagnetism. We have learned to broadcast between our site and the laboratory in Arizona to a particular room in a particular house on a particular corner in Berlin and kept the same kind of data developing there as in our site in Arizona. I will be imprinting it to broadcast to a group of children diagnosed to be autistic and their parents, I call it information medicine. That success will breed success and I'll either get into a lot more trouble or it will open up some opportunity.*

I asked Bill to comment further particularly about entrepreneurial behaviour:

*Certainly, they have a willingness to take risks. In my case I had to be willing to give up when I was seemingly at the peak of my conventional field, in order to make myself vulnerable to make myself do this. I didn't really have any choice because I believe in to* **thy own self be true** *and once you're hooked to that passage,* **it's very important and you believe it, to have a happy fruitful life, you follow your zest**.

FOCUSED INTENTION

## KEY POINTS

- Intention is an essential part of the formula for creating an opportunity for an entrepreneur.
- Human intentionality affects material properties as Tiller has shown.
- Human beings affect their environment, at a sub-atomic level.
- Human thought and emotion affects the quantum energetic field
- Communication to the Field occurs at the sub-atomic level when particles collide and collapse through your sustained intention.
- This has been proven in numerous scientific studies.

# CHAPTER 7

## The Mindset of Success

 *Most people don't affect reality in a consistent way; they believe they cannot do it ...*

EMERITUS PROFESSOR WILLIAM TILLER

The journey that an entrepreneur undertakes is a highly personal experience, in essence to take your inner vision and your creation to the wider world. The space to create entrepreneurial thinking and mindset resides within you. It is not external. It is an unconscious process that is able to be brought to consciousness, with awareness and practice.

Conscious creation is the outcome of aligning with your vision and purpose to ensure that what happens in your life is actually what you want to create. We create most often unconsciously as we do not realise the power of our thoughts and, importantly, our intention. Just as a computer has a hard drive running in the background, your brain is constantly accessing beliefs, memories, and thoughts that are beyond your conscious awareness. In Chapter 6, you read that there is scientific evidence that ultimately proves that we affect material properties and our external world with our thoughts.

Clarity of vision and purpose unlocks the door to success. Finding what gives you joy, what makes your heart sing … that is your passion, is the first step.

What do you really want in your life? And what have you created to date? When you contemplate these questions, what springs to mind? Do you know what is important to you – what your values are – what your beliefs are about your life? Why do you get out of bed in the morning? And what is the first thing you say to yourself when you do? How positive are you? Do you feel stressed every time you think about today or this week? The way in which you **think** about your life affects every aspect and impacts on your relationships with other people through heart and brain entrainment.

Sixty per cent of the neural cells in the heart are identical cells to cells that are in your brain and the heart is more powerful (as a resonator) than your brain. When your brain and heart are in sync, you experience a state of coherence. (see Chapter 2) This increases the potential for you to be able to create consciously what you desire.

If you are feeling unhappy, stressed, under pressure or unwell, it is time to consider how to change what is occurring in your life. Knowing what your unique talents are and having clarity about what you want to create in your life is the key to success.

An entrepreneur's mindset is already wired this way; an individual who is highly intuitive, absolutely passionate, is focused on the outcome they seek and is deliberately intentional in their actions and behaviours constantly scanning their environment for future opportunities and repeatedly creating successful businesses.

Scientists and researchers have known this for many years. What has not been available until now is how to create it, intentionally.

The only barrier to thinking like an entrepreneur and experiencing success is the person staring back at you – in the mirror!

This chapter will enable you to begin practising to think like an entrepreneur.

To review what you have read so far:

- Successful entrepreneurs act on their intuition, trusting it to establish the business vision or initial idea.
- This intuitive action can be measured using electro-physiological tools to test heart rate variability and is achieved by gaining attentional coherence.
- When you create your personal electro-magnetic signature to match one of the potentials in the field, you will be drawn to it or it will find you in your new reality.
- The entrepreneurs' opportunity is created by sustaining their level of passion, with pure intention.
- Being aware that your intention is powerful and that the highest good of all must be done, is critical.
- Let go of the outcome, not worrying about how or what or when it will happen!
- Be grateful when your intention arrives. Acknowledge and give thanks!

When you apply these steps as a formula, intentionally and with passion, it can be observed visually as shown in the following chart.

## The Formula for Entrepreneurial Mindset

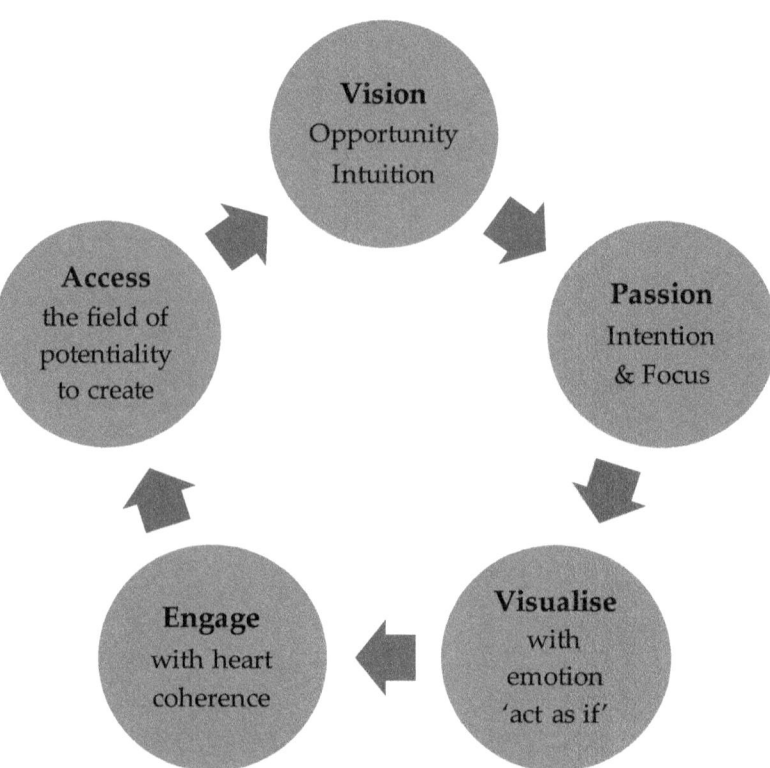

# THE MINDSET OF SUCCESS

Here is a practical technique for you to use to develop your entrepreneurial thinking:

## Practical Technique – Think Like an Entrepreneur

### Stage One

Think of an experience you would passionately wish to create. This affects you, and will serve your and others higher purpose – it is aligned to your values. It is an experience that you can influence, not one that other people directly control. Hold this intention in advance.

You may bring to mind several experiences:

a) One that you would love to create in the near future, say within a week

b) One that you would love to create in the next month to two month period

c) One that you would love to create within the next six months

d) Write your intentions down on a sheet of paper – separate page for each

e) Write your review dates down now in your device or on paper.

### Stage Two: Accessing Coherence

#### Step 1: Heart Focus

Focus your attention on the area around your heart, the area in the centre of your chest. If you prefer, the first couple of times you try it, place your hand over the centre of your chest to help keep your attention in the heart area.

### Step 2: Heart Breathing
Breathe deeply but normally and focus as if your breath is coming in and going out through your heart area. Continue breathing with ease until you find a natural inner rhythm that feels good to you.

### Step 3: Heart Feeling
As you maintain your heart focus and heart breathing, activate a positive feeling. Recall a positive feeling, a time when you felt good inside, and try to re-experience the feeling. One of the easiest ways to generate a positive, heart-based feeling is to remember a special place you've been to or the love you feel for a close friend or family member or treasured pet. This is the most important step.

## Stage Three: Access the Field of Opportunity

Every day, preferably at the same time of day, strongly visualise and intend in a positive manner, by words, thoughts, visualisation and writing in your journal what the experience is that you choose to create, from a state of coherence.

Let your intent strengthen by seeing yourself living your goal, hearing what is being said, feeling what you will feel, the emotion, when you are living your experience.

Know with clarity and certainty that you are attuning yourself to the field of all potentialities and you will draw to you precisely what it is that you wish to create.

Become aware of any negative thoughts/beliefs that may emerge during this process. If this occurs, go back to your intention and re-create a coherent state.

Record in your journal what occurs. Now let go of your intentions until the next time you repeat this exercise. Know that the field of potentialities is responding to you and does not need constant reminders of what you want to create.

Continue to be clear and confident that your new reality is emerging in your life.

Review your diarised dates within one week, one month and six months to review your breakthrough. [i]

---

[i] HeartMath Institute®. *"The Science of the Heart"*. *www.heartmath.org/free-services/tools-for-well-being/quick-coherence-adult.html*

# Afterword

This book has been some time in the womb since its conception. In the time it has taken to interview, sort, develop, research and write it, I have been on my own personal journey, as a serial entrepreneur.

I have lived some of the experiences that people I interviewed for the book had related, for example, I have always had a passionate idea for my business and put my all into it – with intuition and intentionality. And yet I had the experience of a near failure of the business accompanied by a significant health challenge and adrenal burn-out.

So you may ask, what have I learnt, so far on my journey as an entrepreneur.

I have learnt that when I am less than positive in fact downright negative and disempowered, that nothing works! I am not in the zone of coherence. I have learnt that I really do affect my environment and other people sometimes, in a not so good way (enough said!) The single minded approach that a true entrepreneur adopts is often at odds with other people, who simply do not get it! The number of times, well meaning people said, *go and get a normal job* ... exceeds double digits! For me, a normal job does not exist. Perhaps a potential employer picks up the vibes!

I know that I set up my own reality by my thoughts, emotions and intentions. Having spiritual, physical and emotional wellbeing is paramount for me. Employing disciplines such as meditation and stress management is a daily practice.

Silencing the 'monkey mind' recognising what is true and what is not, is critical to my self-esteem; having confidence, trust and faith that moving towards my goal will and does engender it.

I have proven the formula I have written, again and again. I asked some other close friends and colleagues to work with the techniques I have developed. And I ask each one of you to use this formula, provide feedback and add to the growing body of research information.

Simply go to www.janemara.com and add your feedback after working with the techniques as described at the end of Chapter 7.

The journey of an entrepreneur is not an easy one, yet it is the most singularly rewarding one that I can think of.

As Steve Jobs so rightly said:

**"Your time is limited – do not let the noise of others opinions drown out your own inner voice, and have the courage to follow your heart and intuition."**

Be brave – enjoy the ride – follow your heart and your intuition!

# References

Bradley, Raymond Trevor, *The psychophysiology of entrepreneurial intuition: A quantum-holographic theory*, Institute for Whole Social Science; HeartMath Institute®, California, USA and e-Motion Institute, Auckland, New Zealand, Third AGSE International Entrepreneurship Research Exchange, February 8–10, 2006. http://citeseerx.ist.psu.edu/viewdoc/summary?doi=10.1.1.695.1131

Bradley, Raymond Trevor, Institute for Whole Social Science, Institute of HeartMath®, California, USA, e-Motion Institute, Auckland, New Zealand; Murray Gillin, Australian Graduate School of Entrepreneurship; Dana Tomasino, Institute for Whole Social Science, e-Motion Institute. *Transformational Dynamics of Entrepreneurial Systems: The Organizational Basis of Intuitive Action*, Regional Frontiers of Entrepreneurial Research, 2008. https://www.heartmath.org/assets/uploads/2015/01/agse-2008-the-transformational-dynamics-of-entrepreneurship.pdf

Deloitte | AMP Capital, *It's (almost) all about me. Workplace 2030: Built for us,* July 2013. https://www2.deloitte.com/.../deloitte-au-hc-diversity-future-work-amp-2013.pdf

Dispenza, Dr Joe, *Evolve your Brain – The science of changing your mind*, Health Communications, Inc., 2007. http://drjoedispenza.com/index.php?page_id=Evolve-Your-Brain

Dyer, Dr Wayne W, *The Power of Intention*, 1995. http://www.hayhouse.com/the-power-of-intention-5/

Encarta Dictionary, English UK, *Quantum physics* – *The theory describing behaviours and interactions of energy states which proposes that energy is subdivided into discrete amounts and that matter possesses wave properties.*

EOC Institute, *How Brainwave Entrainment with EquiSync® Can Change Your Life.* http://eocinstitute.org/meditation/brainwave_charts_brainwave_patterns

Gillin, Murray; La Pira, Frank; McCraty, Rollin; Bradley, Raymond Trevor, *Before Cognition: The Active Contribution of the Heart / ANS to Intuitive Decision Making as measured on Repeat Entrepreneurs in the Cambridge Technopol.* HeartMath Institute®. www.heartmath.org

Gillin, Murray; La Pira, Frank; McCraty, Rollin; Bradley, Raymond Trevor, *It is the individual's passion or "rapt attention"– biological energy activated in his emotional connection to the object of his interest–that generates the outgoing attentional wave directed to the object of his interest that generates the outgoing attentional wave directed to the object*, HeartMath Institute®. www.heartmath.org

HeartMath Institute®, *Exploring the Role of the Heart in Human Performance.* www.heartmath.org

HeartMath Institute®, *Science of the Heart frequencies: Transition to Entrainment.* www.heartmath.org

HeartMath Institute®, *The Science of the Heart.* www.heartmath.org.

# REFERENCES

HeartMath Institute®, *Solutions for Stress: Developing your intuition.* https://www.heartmath.org/resources/solutions-for-stress/reducing-stress/

HeartMath Institute®, *The Quick Coherence® Technique for Adults.* http://www.heartmath.org/free-services/tools-for-well-being/quick-coherence-adult.html

Jobs, Steve, *Commencement speech at Stanford University.* http://news.stanford.edu/news/2005/june15/jobs-061505.html

Lipton, Dr Bruce, PhD, *The conscious brain accounts for only 5% of our brain's cognitive functionality.* www.brucelipton.com

Loye, 1983; Radin 1997a; Bierman 2000; Spottiswoode 2003, McCraty et al., 2004a, *Intuition is not confined simply to cognitive-based perception, but involves the entire psycho-physiological system often associated with emotional and or physiological responses We believe that such intuition (nonlocal) involves the body's connection to a field of energy beyond normal consciousness).*

Scharmer, Otto, *Theory of U: Leading from the Emerging Future.* MIT Sloan School of Management.

Sheldrake,R upert 1999; McCraty, Rollin et al., 2004b. *A comprehensive study of animal's premonition concluded that pets can sense the return of their owners long before they can see or hear them.*

Shelton, Charlotte K, *Quantum Leaps: 7 Skills for Workplace Recreation*, 1999.

The Concise Oxford Dictionary, UK

Tiller, Dr William A, Institute of Psychoenergetic Science.
www.tillerinstitute.org

# Jane Mara

**AUTHOR, FOUNDER & CEO**
**EXPERT INTUITION PTY LTD**

Jane is a published author, researcher, management consultant and executive coach applying the power of personal mindset to business and life challenges. As a global researcher, she recognised the power of accessing intuition deliberately to produce better insights that directly translated into higher profitability for her clients.

She is highly regarded for dissemination of complex scientific knowledge into practical applications for business. She has contextualised intuitive intelligence into decision-making, resilience strategies for stress management and to develop entrepreneurial thinking.

Jane is well regarded as a speaker/facilitator and coach with the ability to communicate from one-on-one to audiences of hundreds of people.

As the founder/CEO of Expert Intuition, Jane will develop your intuition as a skill expanding personal consciousness to allow more Aha moments, breakthroughs and insights to occur, easily.

## Publications

- *Intuition on Demand*: Activate your Intuitive Intelligence for Business Success, ISBN 0646466232, 2006
- *Think Like an Entrepreneur*: The Mindset of Success, ISBN 9780646974408, 2017

## Contact Details

Jane Mara

jane@janemara.com

www.janemara.com

# What makes an entrepreneur successful?

The latest scientific research revealed in this book demonstrates that entrepreneurial thinking can be easily developed by everyone and is far more than creative thinking, idea generation or brain-storming techniques.

What makes serial entrepreneurs successful is their personal mindset. What is less known is how their internal process develops their mindset to perform at the highest level. And it is much more than their ability to tolerate high risk or failure. The entrepreneur develops their personal mindset from an inner perspective, they trust that clarity will emerge from intuition to inform the initial idea or vision for a business.

This intuition is beyond the brain, it appears in the heart, gut and internal organs. We have a unique intuitive intelligence and you will learn just how entrepreneurs use this information to both attract and create a successful business.

This formula is the GPS for your entrepreneurial success. This formula has never been revealed outside the academic world. Through interviews with scientists, serial entrepreneurs and business thinkers about their individual experiences and with proven application and techniques, Jane Mara has unlocked the key to what makes serial entrepreneurs successful.

Jane Mara's *Think Like an Entrepreneur: The Mindset of Success* demystifies how serial entrepreneurs behave and what it takes to create successful business ventures.

Importantly her research has focused on seeking an understanding of how successful repeat entrepreneurs integrate intuition and intentionality into recognising opportunities for business innovation and development. Jane has proven that this formula is accessible for all who wish to adopt more entrepreneurial thinking.

> ❝ Don't let the noise of others' opinions drown out your own inner voice. And most important, have the courage to follow your heart and intuition.
> Steve Jobs

www.ingramcontent.com/pod-product-compliance
Lightning Source LLC
Chambersburg PA
CBHW040554010526
44110CB00054B/2675